OCT 03

IMMIGRANTS IN AMERICA

Chinese Americans

German Americans

Irish Americans

Italian Americans

Japanese Americans

Swedish Americans

China

- International boundary
- Province-level boundary
- ★ National capital
- ⊙ Province-level capital
- ┼ Railroad
- Road

IMMIGRANTS IN AMERICA

Chinese
AMERICANS

Michael Martin

CHELSEA HOUSE
PUBLISHERS
A Haights Cross Communications Company

Philadelphia

Frontispiece: Map of China with world map inset. Chinese immigrants endured a long and often difficult voyage across the Pacific Ocean for a new and better life in America.

CHELSEA HOUSE PUBLISHERS

VP, New Product Development Sally Cheney
Director of Production Kim Shinners
Creative Manager Takeshi Takahashi
Manufacturing Manager Diann Grasse

Staff for CHINESE AMERICANS

Assistant Editor Kate Sullivan
Production Editor Jaimie Winkler
Picture Researcher Pat Holl
Series Designer Takeshi Takahashi
Cover Designer Takeshi Takahashi
Layout 21st Century Publishing and Communications, Inc.

A Haights Cross Communications ✦ Company

http://www.chelseahouse.com

First Printing

1 3 5 7 9 8 6 4 2

Library of Congress Cataloging-in-Publication Data

Martin, Michael, 1948–
   Chinese Americans / Michael Martin.
      p. cm.—(Immigrants in America)
Includes bibliographical references and index.
   ISBN 0-7910-7126-XHC   07910-7513-3PB
   1. Chinese Americans—History—Juvenile literature. 2. Immigrants—
United States—History—Juvenile literature. 3. China—Emigration and immigration—
History—Juvenile literature. 4. United States—Emigration and immigration—
History—Juvenile literature. [1. Chinese Americans. 2. Immigrants.] I. Title.
II. Series: Immigrants in America (Chelsea House Publishers)
E184.C5 M19 2002
973'.04951—dc21
                                                                    2002151349

CONTENTS

Introduction
Daniel Patrick Moynihan   6

1   The Chinese in America   12

2   The Old Country   24

3   The Journey to the
    Flowery Flag Nation   34

4   Life Across the Pacific   44

5   The "Yellow Peril"   56

6   The Tide Turns   70

7   Into the Melting Pot:
    The Chinese–American Influence   84

    Chronology   98

    Bibliography   101

    Further Reading   103

    Websites   104

    Organizations   105

    Index   106

A NATION OF NATIONS

Daniel Patrick Moynihan

The Constitution of the United States begins: "We the People of the United States . . ." Yet, as we know, the United States was not then and is not now made up of a single group. It is made up of many peoples. Immigrants and bondsmen from Europe, Asia, the Pacific Islands, Africa, and Central and South America came here or were brought here, and still they come. They forged one nation and made it their own. More than 100 years ago, Walt Whitman expressed this great central fact of America: "Here is not merely a nation, but a teeming Nation of nations."

Although the ingenuity and acts of courage of these immigrants, our ancestors, shaped the North American way of life, we sometimes take their contributions for granted. This fine series, IMMIGRANTS IN AMERICA, examines the experiences and contributions of different immigrant groups and how these contributions determined the future of the United States and Canada.

Immigrants did not abandon their ethnic traditions when they reached the shores of North America. Each ethnic group had its own customs and traditions, and each brought different experiences, accomplishments, skills, values, styles of dress, and tastes in food that lingered long after its arrival. Yet this profusion of differences created a bond among immigrants. Ethnic foods, for example, sometimes became "typically" American, such as frankfurters, pizzas, and tacos.

The United States and Canada are unusual in this respect. Whereas religious and ethnic differences have sparked intolerance throughout the rest of the world, North Americans have struggled to learn how to respect each other's differences and live in harmony.

Our two countries are hardly the only two in which different groups must learn to live together. There is no nation of significant size anywhere in the world that would not be classified as multiethnic. But only in North America are there so *many* different groups, most of them living cheek by jowl with one another.

This is not easy. Look around the world. And it has not always been easy for us. Witness the exclusion of Chinese immigrants, and for practical purposes the Japanese also, in the late nineteenth century. But by the late twentieth century, Chinese and Japanese Americans were the most successful of all the groups recorded by the census. We have had prejudice aplenty, but it has been resisted and recurrently overcome.

The remarkable ability of Americans to live together as one people was seriously threatened by the issue of slavery. Thousands of settlers from the British Isles had arrived in the colonies as indentured servants, agreeing to work for a specified number of years on farms or as apprentices in return for passage to America and room and board. When the first Africans arrived in the then-British colonies during the seventeenth century, some colonists thought that they, too, should be treated as indentured servants. Eventually, the question of whether the Africans should be treated as indentured, like the English, or as slaves who could be owned for life, was considered in a Maryland court. The court's calamitous decree held that blacks were slaves bound to a lifelong servitude, and so also were their children. America went through a time of moral examination and civil war before African slaves and their descendants were finally freed. The principle that all people are created equal had faced its greatest challenge and it survived.

Yet the court ruling that set blacks apart from other races fanned flames of discrimination that burned long after slavery was abolished—and that still flicker today. Indeed, it was about the time of the American Civil War that European theories of evolution were turned to the service of ranking different peoples by their presumed distance from our apelike ancestors!

When the Irish flooded American cities to escape the famine in Ireland, the cartoonists caricatured the typical "Paddy" (a common term for Irish immigrants) as an apelike creature with jutting jaw and sloping forehead.

By the twentieth century, racism and ethnic prejudice had given rise to virulent theories of a Northern European master race. When Adolf Hitler came to power in Germany in 1933, he popularized the notion of an Aryan race. Only a man of the deepest ignorance and evil could have done this. *Aryan* is a Sanskrit word taken from the ancient language of the civilizations that inhabited the Indus Valley, which now includes Pakistan and much of Northern India. The term "Aryan," which means "noble," was first used by the eminent German linguist Max Müller to denote the Indo-European family of languages. Müller was horrified that anyone could think of it in terms of a race of blond-haired, blue-eyed Teutons. But the Nazis embraced the notion of a master race. Anyone with darker and heavier features was considered inferior. Buttressed by these theories, the German Nazi state from 1933 to 1945 set out to destroy European Jews, along with Poles, Gypsies, Russians, and other groups considered inferior. They nearly succeeded. Millions of these people were murdered.

The tragedies brought on by ethnic and racial intolerance throughout the world demonstrate the importance of North America's efforts to create a society free of prejudice and inequality.

A relatively recent example of the New World's desire to resolve ethnic friction nonviolently is the solution that the Canadians found to a conflict between two ethnic groups. A long-standing dispute as to whether Canadian culture was properly English or properly French resurfaced in the mid-1960s, dividing the peoples of the French-speaking Province of Quebec from those of the English-speaking provinces. Relations grew tense, then bitter, then violent. The Royal Commission on Bilingualism and Biculturalism was established to study the growing crisis and to propose measures to ease the tensions. As a result of the commission's recommendations, all official documents and statements from the national government's capital at Ottawa are now issued in both French and English, and bilingual education is encouraged. But the commissioners recorded that there were many other groups as well.

Toward the end of the nineteenth century in the United States, public figures such as Theodore Roosevelt began speaking about "Americanism," deploring "hyphenated Americans" as persons only partly assimilated—later it would be said insufficiently loyal—to their adopted country. Ethnicity was seen by many as a threat to national cohesion, and even to national security. During World War I, referring to German Americans, Roosevelt would speak of "the Hun within." During World War II, immigrant Germans and Italians were classified as "enemy aliens," and Japanese Americans were settled in detention camps. With time, however, we became more accepting as ethnicity emerged as a *form* of Americanism, celebrated in the annual Columbus Day and Steuben Day parades, the West Indian parade, the Pakistani parade, and in New York City the venerable St. Patrick's Day parade, which dates back before the American Revolution.

In time, the Bureau of the Census took note. In 1980, for the first time, the census questionnaire asked, "What is this person's ancestry?" In parentheses, it stated: "For example: Afro-American, English, French, German" and so on through a list of 16 possibilities, followed by "etc." The results were a bit misleading. Remember, it was a new question. Census officials now speculate that because the first European group listed was English, many respondents simply stopped there. The result was an "overcount." By 2000, however, the bureau was getting better.

The 2000 census also asked people to identify their ancestry. More than 80 percent chose one or more groups from a list of 89 different groups. Most people "specified," as the census states, a "single ancestry," but almost a quarter cited "multiple ancestry." So which is it: are we a melting pot or a "Nation of nations"? The answer is both. Americans share a common citizenship, which is the most important fact of our civic life. But most also feel part of one group or another, especially recent arrivals.

Of which there are many indeed! Since 1970 more than 26 million immigrants have entered the United States; most immigrants have entered legally, but of late not all. For the longest time, anyone could enter. Under the Constitution, drawn up in 1797, even the trade in African slaves was protected for 20 years—a hideous practice, but well established in Southern states. In time, however, hostility toward newcomers appeared, notably tinged with racial fears. In 1882 an act of U.S. Congress excluded further Chinese immigration, responding to pressure from Californians anxious about "cheap labor." Next there was agitation to exclude Japanese, which only ended when the Japanese government, in what was termed a "Gentleman's Agreement," consented to withhold passports from Japanese emigrants. Restrictions on Asians continued until 1965.

Indeed, at the end of the nineteenth century there was much talk about the "Anglo-Saxon race" and its many virtues. The United States had reached an informal alliance with Great Britain, and we were setting up an empire of our own that included the Philippines, Cuba, Puerto Rico, and Hawaii. Weren't we different from those "others"? Not exactly. Migration has been going on across the world from the beginning of time and there is no such thing as a pure race. The humorist Finley Peter Dunne wrote: "An Anglo-Saxon…is a German that's forgot who was his parents." Indeed, following the departure of the Romans from Britain in the year A.D. 410, Germanic tribes, including Saxons from northern Germany and Anglos from southern Denmark, migrated into the British Isles. In time they defined what we now call Britain, driving the Celts to Wales and Ireland, with an essentially Celtic Scotland to the north.

Thus immigrants from the British Isles, approximately a third of the present day population of the United States, were already a heterogeneous group. Perhaps even more importantly, they belonged to many different religious denominations including the Puritan, Congregational, Episcopalian, Quaker, and Catholic churches, and even a small community of Sephardic Jews from Brazil! No group made up a majority; religious toleration came about largely because there seemed to be no alternative.

American immigration policy developed in much this way. Though completely open at the beginning, over time, efforts were made to limit the influx of certain immigrant groups, in the manner of the exclusion of Asians in the late nineteenth century and the Southern Europeans by the early twentieth century. By the 1960s, however, America was already too diverse to pretend otherwise, and immigration was opened to all nations.

The people of North America are the descendants of one of the greatest migrations in history. And that migration is not over. Koreans, Vietnamese, Mexicans, Nicaraguans, Pakistanis, Indians, Arabs, and many others are heading for the shores of North America in large numbers. This mix of cultures shapes every aspect of our lives. To understand ourselves, we must know something about our diverse ethnic ancestry. Nothing so defines the North American nations as the motto on the Great Seal of the United States: *E Pluribus Unum*—Out of Many, One. ■

1 THE CHINESE IN AMERICA

There were four in our family, my mother, my father, my sister, and me. We lived in a two room house. Our sleeping room and the other served as a parlor, kitchen and dining room. We were not rich enough to keep pigs or fowls; otherwise, our small house would have been more than overcrowded

How can we live on six baskets of rice which were paid twice a year for my father's duty as a night watchman? Sometimes the peasants have a poor crop then we go hungry . . . sometimes we went hungry for days. My mother and me would go over the harvested rice fields of the peasants to pick the grains they dropped . . . we had only salt and water to eat with the rice.

—An immigrant describing the conditions
that led to his coming to the United States in the 1850s

Chinese and Filipino workers lay railroad tracks for the Burlington Railroad in Washington State in 1959. Chinese men, who were never allowed to become citizens, built a significant number of the railroads that united the country.

From 1865 to 1869, more than 10,000 Chinese immigrants, many of them just off the boat from China, endured incredible hardships while completing what would be called the greatest engineering feat of the nineteenth century. Ironically, although they would never become citizens of the United States, these hard-working young men who were trying to escape the poverty of China did as much to unite the country as any other ethnic group. The Transcontinental Railroad was a vital first step in turning the United States into the mighty industrial giant it would soon become.

THE TRANSCONTINENTAL RAILROAD

Pushing eastward from Sacramento, California, the mostly Chinese crews of the Central Pacific Railroad planned to eventually join up with crews working westward from Omaha, Nebraska. Once completed, the Transcontinental Railroad would be the longest continuous railway in the world. Yet many of the best engineers of the day sincerely doubted the project could ever be completed. Their feeling was that there was no way that a railway could be blasted over and through the unbelievably rugged terrain of the Sierra Nevada and Rocky Mountains east of Sacramento, California. The men who owned the Central Pacific Railroad gambled otherwise. But by the winter of 1864, even they had their doubts. After two years of work, only 50 miles of track had been laid—and that was over some of the flattest terrain of the entire route.

Finding qualified labor was the biggest problem. In an age before earth-moving machines, railroad building was back-breaking pick-and-shovel work that hardly anyone cared to do. In labor-scarce California, the Central Pacific had advertised for 5,000 laborers, but only 600 had signed on. And the white men it did hire had an annoying tendency to leave the job after their first payday. Whenever word of gold or silver being discovered in the nearby mountains reached them, they'd quit with the hope of striking it rich. Almost as bad, most of these rough-and-tumble men drank heavily. Drunken brawls, as well as fights and even murders, were common. It was not an atmosphere where much progress could be made.

Finally, someone suggested hiring Chinese workers. At the time, there were several thousand Chinese in California. They had begun arriving in the state around the time of the Gold Rush some 15 years before. At first, there was great resistance to hiring non-whites. The feeling was that they were not strong enough to handle the work. Then, in desperation, the Central Pacific hired 50 Chinese on a trial basis. Charles Crocker, the Central Pacific's construction boss, was surprised by the results.

"They prove nearly equal to the white men in the amount of labor they perform," he reported enthusiastically, "and are much more reliable." It did not take long to discover that, even though few spoke English, the Chinese had a rare ability to learn on the job. They soon became experts at grading, drilling, masonry, and demolition.

Before long, the Central Pacific was hiring every Chinese worker it could find. At one point, a fourth of all the Chinese in America were working on the railroad. When the Central Pacific ran out of immigrants to hire, it advertised in China, encouraging young men to cross the Pacific and sign up for the project. In time, 15,000 Chinese would be on the Central Pacific's payroll. Meanwhile, over the next four years, Crocker's admiration for the Chinese increased, particularly after the line reached the High Sierras and an obstacle called Cape Horn.

CONQUERING CAPE HORN

In the High Sierras, a huge a wall of stone loomed above a narrow gorge on the North Fork of the American River. The nearly perpendicular cliff rose some 2,000 feet. Somehow, a ledge for the railway would have to be carved out of solid rock. At this point, a Chinese interpreter saved the day. He approached James Strobridge, superintendent of the project, and explained that the Chinese had developed ways of working on the difficult terrain.

Strobridge was desperate enough to give their method a try. The Chinese worked in teams of three. From the top of the precipice, two men lowered a third man in a reed basket fastened with ropes. Suspended in midair, the man in the basket chipped away with a hammer until he could drill a hole. When he'd made enough room for a charge, he inserted blasting powder. Then he lit the fuse and hoped he could be raised out of harm's way before the charge went off. It was death-defying work. Sometimes the dynamite went off too early; sometimes the ropes broke. Despite casualties, the work continued day after day.

For an entire summer and fall and on into the winter, the

Chinese dangled from their ropes, chipping away at a mountain of rock. When they finished, the roadbed they'd carved out of Cape Horn was considered one of the wonders of the entire Central Pacific line. It was not, however, recommended for anyone with a fear of heights. As one writer put it, "The finest view is at Cape Horn but the sight is not good for nervous people."

Cape Horn cost many Chinese lives. And many more would be lost in the years ahead. Between 1865 and 1869, at least 1,200 bodies were shipped back to China, but the death toll was undoubtedly much higher. With so many deaths occurring from explosions, falls and avalanches, many bodies were never found. Some of the most difficult work occurred high in the mountains after Cape Horn was conquered.

Plans called for the drilling of more than a dozen tunnels, each at least 1,000 feet long. Teams chipped away at the granite in 8-hour shifts, 24 hours a day. They worked on 10 different tunnels simultaneously. The longest—almost 1,700 feet—was called the Summit Tunnel. Although workers used up to 500 kegs of blasting powder per day to carve out Summit Tunnel, they cleared little more than a foot of rock every 24 hours. In fact, working from both ends and from the middle (a shaft was sunk into the mountain), it took over a year to carve out the entire tunnel!

Meanwhile, the Sierras were experiencing two of the worst winters in history. At times, crews battled snowdrifts that were 40 feet deep. By January, they gave up trying to keep paths open between the line and the camps. Instead, they dug tunnels beneath the snow. Using shafts for air and lanterns for light, 3,000 Chinese lived like moles for months, passing from work to their living quarters in the dim half-light far below the snow's surface.

As snow accumulated on the upper ridges, the thunderous roar of avalanches was heard more and more often. Moments later, a work crew or even an entire camp might go hurtling down the mountainside. Not until spring, if at all, were the bodies recovered. Some workers were found with picks and shovels still clutched in their frozen hands.

Despite such incredible hardships, the indomitable Chinese pushed on. After they passed out of the mountains, the work, unfortunately, did not get any easier. The two railroads—the Central Pacific and the Union Pacific—were racing toward each other as fast as they could. There was good reason for their haste. For each mile of track completed, Congress had set aside land and money for the railroad that built it. Since time was money, the Central Pacific bosses pushed their workers mercilessly. In 1868 alone, the workers laid 362 miles of track.

COMPLETION OF THE RAILROAD

By the spring of 1869, as the two railroads neared each other in Utah, a competition developed between the crews of the Union Pacific and the Central Pacific. Most of the Union Pacific laborers were Irish, whereas Chinese laborers made up 90 percent of the Central Pacific work force. The Irish laborers vowed not to be outdone by "a bunch of Chinamen." One day they would lay six miles of track; the next day the Chinese would lay seven. On April 27, the one-day record stood at 7.5 miles and was held by the Union Pacific crews. Starting the next morning, the Central Pacific and its Chinese laborers demonstrated once and for all their mastery of the railroad building process. In 12 hours, they laid over 10 miles of track by hand. That day 125 tons of rails were laid—a record that will probably stand for all time.

On May 10, 1869, the final spike joining the two railroads was scheduled to be put in place at Promontory, Utah. The event was the nineteenth century's equivalent of putting a man on the moon. The entire country was eager for the details. As the last spike—a golden spike specially made for the occasion—was driven, a telegraph operator sitting at a table set up beside the track tapped out the news to the entire nation.

On May 10, 1869, employees and officials celebrate as the Union Pacific and Central Pacific railroads connect in Promontory, Utah. Absent from the photograph are the Chinese men who did much of the labor.

LACK OF RECOGNITION TOWARD CHINESE WORKERS

Meanwhile, reporters and photographers, as well as leaders of business and government, had gathered at Promontory for days. Many famous photographs were taken that day, yet the Chinese laborers who actually built the railroad are noticeably absent from them. Many speeches were given afterward, thanking all who had made this great feat possible, yet almost no one mentioned the Chinese. The exception was Charles Crocker. "In the midst of our rejoicing," he noted, "I wish to call to mind that the early completion of this railroad we have built has been in great measure due to that poor destitute class of laborers called the Chinese, to the fidelity and industry they have shown . . . "

The lack of recognition for their accomplishments was something Chinese immigrants would experience again and again during their first 100 years in the United States. Although they literally helped to build this country, their considerable contributions were mostly ignored. What was even worse, they faced kinds of discrimination and prejudice that no other ethnic group has ever had to face.

DISCRIMINATION AND THE EXCLUSION ACT

Laws were passed forbidding Chinese to own land, to vote or even join a union. Because they were neither black nor white, they were denied the opportunity to become citizens. Restrictions were placed on where they could live; judges ruled that their word could not be used in courts of law. If a white man murdered a Chinese man and the only witnesses were Chinese, then the white man was allowed to go free because, it was claimed, no Chinese could be expected to tell the truth. In 15 states, a white person could be put in prison for the "crime" of marrying a Chinese person.

Then, only 13 years after the last spike of the Transcontinental Railroad was driven, Congress passed the Exclusion Act of 1882. It drastically banned the immigration of Chinese laborers to the United States, something that had never been done before to any immigrant group. For 61 years, the law remained in effect. During that time, especially during the last two decades of the nineteenth century, Chinese immigrants in the United States were also subject to innumerable acts of violence and lawlessness. Mobs of whites often attacked any Chinese people they saw on the streets. Many other Chinese were murdered and driven from their homes.

IMMIGRATION CONTINUES

Despite the persecution they faced, Chinese immigrants continued coming to America—in most cases to join family members already here. They entered both legally and illegally. Things began to change for the better after 1943 when the Exclusion Act was repealed. Immigration restrictions were eased and Chinese could become U.S. citizens. Changing

My America

When Tung Pok Chin arrived in the United States in the 1930s, maintaining a false identity was still one of the few ways that Chinese could enter the country. This method of entry required strong nerves and a great deal of study.

"I arrived in the United States in Boston in 1934 at the age of nineteen. I had purchased my 'paper,' designating me the son of an American native, on the Chinese black market, and would automatically become a United States citizen upon verification of the facts. For months before leaving China, I studied these 'facts': my paper name, my paper father's name, my paper mother's name, my age, their ages, my place of birth, their place of birth, their occupations, and so on.

This was not easy. I had to completely block out my real and immediate family: my parents who raised me and arranged a marriage for me at the age of thirteen, my wife, my two young sons, aged four and five at the time of my arrival in Boston, and all else that related to them. One slip during the interrogation and I would be sent back on the next boat to China!"

M. Elaine Mar was only a first grader when she arrived in America in 1972. Although she had been praised for being such a bright child back in China, the fact that she could not speak English made her first years in school a nightmare—even though she attended with her American cousin, San.

"Mrs. Tate wrote the equation in big chalk figures on the board. She asked for a volunteer. The more enthusiastic students raised their hands. Mrs. Tate scanned the room, then decided, 'Let's give Elaine a chance.' I didn't understand a word, not even my new name. There was silence. 'Elaine?' Mrs. Tate repeated. I didn't respond. 'That's your name,' San reminded me. My classmates started giggling. 'Oh,' I said. I immediately knew the answer, but I couldn't think of the word for 'seven' in English. 'Um,' I said. The children laughed some more. . . .

I felt trapped inside my body. Language seemed a purely physical limitation. Thoughts existed inside my head, but I wasn't able to make them into words. As a consequence, I was forced to observe my classmates from a place inside myself. And the kids just laughed, not able to see beyond my physical shell. They had no idea who I was beyond the mute, lifeless form in the classroom."

In one of many anti-Chinese riots, crowds in Denver, Colorado attacked Chinese buildings and their residents on October 31, 1880. Chinese immigrants endured many acts of violence in the last two decades of the nineteenth century.

attitudes were also reflected in the War Brides Act of 1945. This law allowed 6,000 Chinese women who had married American servicemen to enter the country and become citizens.

Despite increasing immigration after World War II, the number of Chinese on the mainland of the United States—Hawaii has long had a substantial Chinese population—was never more than 200,000 before 1960. But, after President

Johnson signed a new immigration law in 1965, the number of Chinese in the United States rose rapidly.

GROWTH OF CHINESE-AMERICAN POPULATION

Between 1990 and 2000, America's Chinese population nearly doubled. According to the 2000 census, there are now more than

Chinese Immigration in Numbers

Chinese Immigration by decade, courtesy of the United States Immigration and Naturalization Service.

Decade	Number of Immigrants
1821–1830	2
1831–1840	8
1841–1850	35
1851–1860	41,397
1861–1870	64,301
1871–1880	123,201
1881–1890	61,711
1891–1900	14,799
1901–1910	20,605
1911–1920	21,278
1921–1930	29,907
1931–1940	4,928
1941–1950	16,709
1951–1960	9,657
1961–1970	34,764
1971–1980	124,326
1981–1990	346,747
1991–2000	419,114
TOTAL	1,333,489

The entrance to Philadelphia's Chinatown boldly displays the bright colors and traditional designs of the Chinese culture. The Chinese have become the largest Asian ethnic group in the United States, influencing many aspects of American society and culture, from the foods we eat to the movies we see.

2.4 million Chinese living in the United States. They have become the largest Asian ethnic group in this country. From their ranks have emerged leaders in education, entertainment, literature, science, politics, sports, architecture, and many other fields. Further evidence of their successful assimilation into American culture is the prevalence of Chinese cuisine and customs and the growing familiarity with age-old Chinese practices such as acupuncture and Taoism. It may have taken a long time but, just like those indomitable laborers on the Central Pacific Railroad, Chinese Americans overcame mountains of obstacles to become a valued part of a nation they helped to build.

2

THE OLD COUNTRY

PHYSICAL FEATURES AND EARLY HISTORY

Geographically, the United States and China have much in common. Both countries are vast (China is slightly larger), and both have an astonishing variety of climates and landscapes. Like the United States, some regions of China have a tropical climate, and other areas are so cold that the ground never completely thaws. One of the world's driest deserts, three of the world's longest rivers, and the world's highest mountain range all are part of China.

With an area of 3,705,392 square miles (5,963,458 square kilometers), China is the third largest country in the world. Only Russia and Canada have more land. Unfortunately, much of China's land is too mountainous, too dry, or too wet for farming. Only 10 percent of the country is suitable for growing crops. That simple fact has caused much turmoil during China's long history—

The Great Wall of China stretches for 1,500 miles (2,414 kilometers) across the country's north. This impressive wall, the only man-made structure visible from the moon, was built to prevent foreign tribes from attacking the country.

particularly during periods of overpopulation or drought.

Compared with a young nation like the United States, China's history is almost too vast to contemplate. For approximately 4,000 years, the country's culture and institutions have existed in much the same form. During most of that time

China was governed by a series of dynasties. Male rulers, called emperors, passed their power on to sons or other close relatives at the time of their deaths. The first dynasty for which written records survive was the Shang Dynasty. It began about 1,600 years before Christ was born. The last dynasty, the Qing, ended in 1911.

During most of China's recorded history, the country has been isolated from much of the world. Its physical boundaries partially account for that. With an ocean to the east, impassable mountains in the south, and a forbidding desert on the west, it was difficult to travel from China to other countries. Much of China's isolation has been self-imposed. In addition to the geographical barriers to the country's east, south, and west, China's leaders erected one of the most monumental structures in history to the country's north. The Great Wall of China is truly one of the great wonders of the world. Its construction began 23 centuries ago, yet it is so huge that astronauts reported that it was the only man-made structure they could see from the moon.

GREAT WALL OF CHINA

Stretching for 1,500 miles (2,400 kilometers) across northern China, the wall runs from the Yellow Sea in the east to Gansu Province on the west. It is roughly 25 feet high and 15 to 30 feet thick at the base; the top of the wall has a 13-foot roadway running along it. Watchtowers and guard stations were placed at regular intervals so that soldiers could watch for invaders.

The purpose of the wall was to keep out marauding (raiding) tribes that sometimes invaded China from the north. Begun in the third century B.C., it has been expanded many times. Hundreds of thousands of workers (many who died in the process) helped construct it. Surprisingly, the wall seems to have had little military value; despite its existence, a number of invasions from the north were successful. Still, it is a vivid symbol of Chinese ingenuity and serves as a reminder of ancient Chinese attitudes toward the rest of the world.

CHINA'S CLASS SYSTEM

Chinese ruling classes believed their civilization was the most advanced in the world. They saw no need to associate with people they called "barbarians." Up until the 1800s, they had little contact with non-Chinese.

Within China itself, there are at least 56 different ethnic groups. The Han Chinese, comprising 94 percent of the population, have always been the most prominent. Although all of China has one written language, there are so many different dialects that people from different villages often cannot understand one another.

Songs of Gold Mountain

The Canton region of China has a long tradition of folk songs and rhyming poems. It is also the area from which most Chinese immigrants to America came before 1965. That exodus inspired hundreds of new songs and poems. These were known as "Songs of Gold Mountain." Many, like the one about Angel Island below, describe the anguish felt by those detained by immigration authorities. The author of this poem compared his plight with that of a convict forced to wear a cangue (two locked wooden boards with holes for the neck and hands).

The wooden cell is like a steel barrel.
Firmly shut, not even a breeze can filter through.
Over a hundred cruel laws, hard to list them all:
Ten thousand grievances, all from the tortures day and night.
Worry, and more worry—
How can I sleep in peace, eat at ease:
There isn't a cangue, but the hidden punishment is just as weighty.
Tears soak my clothes; frustration fills my bosom.

CHINESE SOCIAL STRUCTURE

Most Chinese have always lived in villages. Even though China has a large population and some very large cities, it remains a largely rural society. In both cities and villages, the basic unit of Chinese culture has always been the family. A typically close-knit Chinese family, however, was much more than just parents and children. It included grandparents, uncles, aunts, and cousins as well as all one's ancestors. In addition, large groups of extended families (or clans) able to trace their roots back to a common ancestor also considered themselves kin. It was not unusual in nineteenth-century China to find that all the residents of a particular village considered themselves members of the same extended family.

The family was also important for keeping order in Chinese society. The head of the family, usually the father, made most of the important decisions. As long as the taxes were paid each year, the central government tended to stay out of local matters. That increased the family's role.

For most of its history, China has been a class society. Under the ruling dynasty, there were four classes—scholar-officials, farmers, artisans, and merchants. Scholar-officials were considered to have the most social value. The brightest children aspired to go into government service. The farmer class, to which most Chinese citizens belonged, was also highly regarded because it provided the food necessary for survival. Meanwhile, of the four classes, merchants had the least prestige.

No matter which class or clan one belonged to, it was possible to also belong to a *hui kuan*. These mutual aid societies were made up of groups of clans from the same region or clans that spoke a similar dialect. Since virtually every Chinese city dweller considered his or her true home to be the rural village or district where they were born, *hui kuans* existed in almost every Chinese city.

Although a newcomer might not be able to find kinsmen

Terraced rice paddies loom over a village in southern China. Even with a high population and several large cities, China has remained a mostly rural society.

in the city, he could count on the *hui kuan* to help him locate those who hailed from the same area, who spoke his native dialect, and who understood his needs and desires. This same strategy for adjusting to new circumstances would be adopted by Chinese who moved to other countries.

Another kind of organization that would one day be

"exported" to other countries was the secret society. Secret societies were groups of desperate men who banded together in search of wealth, power, or protection against corrupt officials or gangs of robbers. Secret societies were alternatives to membership in a clan. Sometimes a man would be expelled from a clan—usually for a criminal behavior of some sort. Without the protection of the clan, he would be easy prey for other criminals or corrupt officials who wanted his possessions.

Like gang members in American cities today, secret society members banded together. They swore an oath of brotherhood to one another. But the members of secret societies were not just criminals. In times of turmoil, farmers, soldiers and merchants might join a secret society to fight against a government they felt was oppressing them.

RELIGION

Such rebellions were not encouraged by Taoism. One of China's major religions, it was based on writings attributed to Lao Zi in the sixth century B.C. Taoists believed in seeking harmony with the forces of nature. The ideal Taoist society would not need many rules, since people living in harmony with nature would naturally live in harmony with everyone around them.

Confucius, a scholar who lived about 500 years before Christ, also instructed his followers on how to achieve a just and harmonious society. He stressed strict obedience to a detailed code of conduct. Although his beliefs, called Confucianism, were more a practical philosophy of life than an actual religion, they have had a huge and lasting influence on Chinese culture. In the years since his death, annual religious ceremonies have been conducted in his honor.

CORRUPTION AND POVERTY

No matter what religion one believed in, harmony was in short supply by the beginning of the nineteenth century when the ruling Qing dynasty was rapidly losing the support of its people. Corrupt officials were stealing money—one of the emperor's top officials amassed a personal fortune of over $1 billion. At the same time, the military was poorly trained and poorly led. And, because it was not keeping up with the pace of military technology taking place in the Western world, it would prove to be no match for the forces soon to invade China.

Meanwhile, at a time when the population was increasing and the food supply shrinking, corrupt officials stole funds set aside for the repair of dikes and dams. In a country where good land was scarce and irrigation was crucial for producing food, the results were disastrous. Both floods and droughts became more damaging, shrinking good cropland even further. Starvation was becoming common.

WARS AND REBELLIONS

Many families could not raise enough to feed themselves, let alone pay taxes. Yet, to maintain the income they had become used to, the rulers raised taxes on everyone else. As the oppression of the people increased, secret societies began increasing membership, and their opposition to the government grew more violent. The government was forced to put down several rebellions that cost millions of lives.

Then, in 1839, the first of the Opium Wars broke out between China and Great Britain. The British wanted to sell opium to the Chinese people against the wishes of the Chinese government. When Chinese troops seized and destroyed a huge shipment of opium, Great Britain declared war, claiming that British rights had been violated. Because the Chinese had few warships and no modern weapons, they lost the war. The British made the Chinese government pay for the war and then began shipping tons of opium into the country.

These humiliations further eroded loyalty to the Qing

Men unload bales of opium from a ship in Hong Kong's harbor. The Chinese government's refusal to allow Great Britain to continue selling opium to the Chinese spurred the first of the Opium Wars in 1839.

Dynasty. Millions were starving, and the people had little faith that their government was capable of improving the situation. More rebellions broke out.

Then, in 1848, amid all this civil disorder, electrifying news reached southeastern China from the other side of the Pacific. Gold had been discovered in a place called California. One of the first men to strike it rich there was a Chinese merchant named Chum Ming, who'd arrived in San Francisco in 1847. Ming sent news of his good fortune back to his village in Guangdong. Such news spread like wildfire, as did the story of two lucky Chinese who found a 40-pound nugget worth $30,000 at a place called Moore's Flat in what is now the State of California. Suddenly, more and more desperate young Chinese men began thinking about leaving home and sailing across 7,000 miles of ocean to Gold Mountain, the Chinese term for the land, rich in gold, that they hoped to find on America's West Coast.

3

THE JOURNEY TO THE FLOWERY FLAG NATION

GOLD FEVER IN GUANGDONG

Guangdong, China's southernmost province was where California gold fever struck the hardest—and for good reasons. Guangdong had always been a hard place to grow food. Every nook and cranny was used for crops, but in times of great economic and political disorder there was never enough. In addition, during the nineteenth century, Guangdong had one of the fastest-growing populations in all of China.

Separated from the rest of China by mountain ranges and hemmed in by the sea, the people of Guangdong have traditionally been more outward-looking than the rest of their countrymen. The province has a long tradition of seafaring and possesses fine natural harbors where great cities such as Guangzhou (Canton) have sprung up. Those harbors allowed

The Pearl River created a natural harbor for Guangzhou (Canton) in the province of Guangdong. As the site of trade, the harbor exposed the people of Guangdong to other cultures. The worldly attitude Guandong's people developed seems to explain why, up until 1965, over 90 percent of Chinese immigrants arriving in the United States came from Guangdong.

for much greater contact with the outside world than the rest of China.

Exposed to other cultures through the foreign ships and the goods they brought, the people of Guangdong were more receptive to the idea of change than most Chinese. Noting that the people of the area were forced by geography to be self-sufficient, Jen Yu Wen, founder of the Guangdong Institute of Culture in Canton, declared that the "people of Kwangtung [Guandong] acquired the qualities of pioneers, growing more adventurous, energetic, independent, and nationalistic."

In fact, between 1840 and 1900, an estimated 2.5 million residents of Guangdong embarked on the ultimate adventure. Leaving their homes to make their living overseas, they sailed aboard ships bound for Southeast Asia, Africa, Australia, The Philippines, New Zealand, Hawaii, and the continental United States. Up until 1965, between 90 and 95 percent of all the Chinese who entered the United States could trace their origins to the Pearl River Delta (another name for the area around Canton).

LEAVING HOME

Great civil unrest during the 1850s and 1860s contributed to the popularity of immigration. The Taipeng Revolution (1851–1864) was said to have taken 25 million lives. During the fighting, rebels from the south devastated the estates of Viceroy Yeh Ming Shen. In the summer of 1855, Shen took revenge on the people of Guangdong. At the public execution grounds in Canton, he had 75,000 people beheaded, most of whom had not even participated in the rebellion.

It took horrors like the mass execution to get many Chinese to even consider leaving their homes and the support provided by their family and clan. Mary Roberts Coolidge, author of *Chinese Immigration*, summed it up for those who made the decision between 1849 and 1882 this way:

> In spite of a dense population and great poverty, the united restraints of law, religion and family ties holds them to the land of their birth and only the greatest stress of war and devastation at home, coincident with the lure of gold and marvelous industrial opportunity in California, served to uproot the three hundred thousand who came to the Pacific Coast during the [first] thirty-three years of free immigration.

One descendant of an immigrant explained: "We were very, very much in debt because of the local warfare. We planted each year, but we were robbed. We had to borrow. When news about the Gold Rush in California was spread by the shippers, my father decided to take a big chance."

Most of the early immigrants were young men, and most were married. Wives and daughters were almost always left behind because it was thought too expensive to support them abroad. Also, in a culture in which family was considered the basis of the social order, keeping immigrants' wives at home guaranteed that they would not forget their kin back in China. They would continue sending money home until they had saved enough to return to their native villages. The following is a Chinese immigrant's unmailed letter, discovered in a drawer at the Kam Wah Chung Store in Oregon:

> It has been several autumns now since your dull husband left you for a far remote alien land. Thanks to my hearty body I am all right. Therefore stop your embroidering worries about me.
>
> Yesterday I received another of your letters. I could not keep tears from running down my cheeks when thinking about the miserable and needy circumstances of our home, and thinking back to the time of our separation.
>
> Because of our destitution I went out, trying to make a living. Who could know that the Fate is always opposite to man's design? Because I can get no gold, I am detained in this secluded corner of a strange land.

The dream of most immigrants was that they would work abroad until they had made their fortune, then return to China to retire as wealthy men. They would then be honored by the grateful families they had kept intact over the years with the earnings they sent home. The knowledge that their income was helping their families survive back in China sustained immigrants through the tough times they would endure once they reached America.

Upon penalty of death, the emperor forbade Chinese citizens from emigrating. They risked being beheaded upon their return to China. But for men desperate enough to think about leaving their homes and families, the emperor's ban was the least of their worries. In addition, they knew that it was almost impossible to enforce.

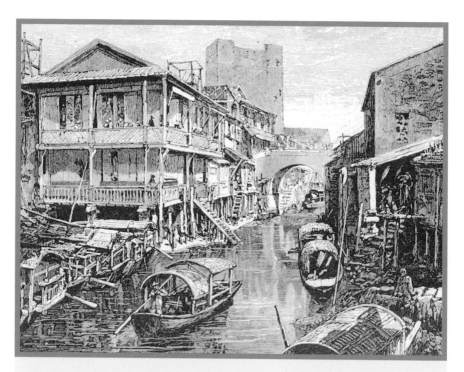

Small boats line a Canton canal. Young men who wanted to emigrate would travel in similar small boats to cities like Canton, Hong Kong, and Macao, where they would board ships bound for America.

THE TRIP

Once the decision to cross the ocean had been made, young men left their native villages and traveled by small boat on the waterways of the Pearl River Delta. To ensure the probability of a safe voyage, they usually tried to get underway before dawn (lessening the chance that they'd meet someone who might utter unlucky words that could endanger the trip). Few carried more than bedding and a bamboo basket with netting over the top. Inside were all their possessions—shoes, hat, and food for the trip.

In sampans, junks, and other small boats, the Chinese emigrants made their way to cities such as Canton, Hong Kong, and Macao. While waiting for their ships to sail, they would stay at one of the *hak-chans*, inns especially designed for holding travelers on their way overseas. Each *hak-chan* special-ized in providing lodging for peasants from a certain area.

FORCED LABOR

In the meantime, however, the emigrants had to avoid the "pig traders." By the middle of the nineteenth century, slavery was coming to an end in most of the world (the United States would be one of the last countries to outlaw it). Now, more than ever, nations like Britain and Spain still needed cheap labor to work in the fields and mines of their colonies. The solution for many was to recruit unknowing young Chinese peasants to work in Peru, Cuba, Hawaii, Jamaica, and other places in the Caribbean and South America. These unsuspecting farmers were tricked or bullied into signing contracts that made them little better than slaves.

The Chinese who refused to sign such contracts were often simply kidnapped or "shanghaied" (the term came from the port of Shanghai). Herded into "pigpens," they were forcibly held before being shipped off to South America or the Caribbean. During the long journeys, they were often starved in order to break their spirit. After they arrived at their destination, the Chinese were forced to work on plantations and in mines under the watch of armed guards. Many thousands died during the journey (of the 140,000 men forced to endure the trip to Cuba, for example, 16,000 died en route) and many more died from the brutal conditions they faced afterward. The unfortunate Chinese who fell victim to this kind of forced labor came to be called "coolies."

BOUND FOR AMERICA

Meanwhile, the Chinese who avoided the gangs of kidnappers booked passage on ships bound for America. Most of the ships that made the run across the Pacific were from Great Britain or the United States. At a time when few peasants made $20 in an entire year, passage to America cost around $50. Some travelers, especially during the 1850s and 1860s, arranged loans from their families or from neighbors.

Later on, the "credit ticket system" developed. Under this arrangement, a merchant paid for an emigrant's ticket. In return, the emigrant agreed to work for a set number of years until the debt was paid. The system was virtually the same as the one used by European immigrants who came to the New World as indentured servants. Repayment of their debts was the first order of business for most Chinese immigrants. They knew that if they did not do so, word of their failure would get back to China and bring great shame on their families.

Travel by sea in the nineteenth century was dangerous and uncomfortable even under the best of conditions. And, because the great sailing ships were dependent on the wind, the 7,000-mile trip to California took anywhere from 51 days to over 100 days. The average trip was about two months, but in 1856 an American ship that encountered unfavorable winds took 115 days. Later, after 1867, when steamships began replacing sailing ships, the time at sea dropped to weeks rather than months.

Conditions aboard ship varied greatly, but in general were quite unpleasant. Chinese almost always traveled in the cheap steerage section, where overcrowding was common. Some ships were so full that immigrants had to take turns sleeping in the same bed. Few passengers were allowed on deck during the voyage. The food was bland and water was limited. Chinese immigrant Huie Kin describes his trip to America in 1868:

> We were two full months or more on our way. . . . When the wind was good and strong, we made much headway. But for days there would be no wind . . . and the ship would drift idly on the smooth sea. . . . Occasionally head winds became so strong as to force us back. Once we thought we were surely lost. . . . Fresh water was scarce and was carefully rationed. Not a drop was allowed to be wasted for washing our faces; and so, when rain came, we eagerly caught the rainwater and did our washing.

Tracing Your Roots

If you are interested in tracing your Chinese roots, there are a variety of resources to help you research and record your family history. Begin in the present and work into the past, taking accurate and organized notes while you research. Although the names of your ancestors are the most important record on the family tree you will create, it is necessary to add details to distinguish your family members from others.

Detailed records are organized by family groups, sets of parents and their children. This includes birth, marriage, and death dates and their locations for each person. It is possible to print blank charts from genealogy research websites, or you can use free online or downloadable genealogy record programs instead.

Start from your memory, listing yourself, your parents, and your siblings on your blank family group record. Many records such as census, land titles, and birth, marriage, and death certificates list information by county as well as city. Always include county information as you compile your records. Then begin a new family group record for each of your parents, listing their siblings and their parents. Once you have listed as much information as you can remember, ask your relatives to fill in any blanks. It is easiest to work on one family line at a time, such as your maternal grandfather's family.

Your living relatives are a valuable source of information. Their memories and stories are a meaningful part of your family tree. They also will have a great deal of information recorded in family bibles, diaries, letters, photographs, birth certificates, marriage licenses, deeds, wills, and obituary clippings. As you fill in your record, list whether the source of information was a letter, a conversation with your grandmother, or information from your great-uncle's military discharge papers that were stored in the attic. This will make it easier to verify your information.

Local history centers and genealogy societies specialize in assisting people in compiling records and have searchable data such as microfilm census records. Your local library also has many resources. The Internet has made it easy to research your family from home, and there are hundreds of websites for genealogists to access particular information. Many sites allow researchers documenting the same family lines to share their files with another. It is always important to double-check the sources others used to find their information so that you can be sure that your ancestors are truly the same.

On a clear, crisp, September morning . . . the mists lifted, and we sighted land for the first time since we left the shores of Kwangtung [Guangdong] over sixty days before. To be actually at the "Golden Gate" of the land of our dreams!

Some vessels ran into storms and vanished without a trace. Because of overcrowding, diseases spread rapidly and sickness and death were common.

When the *Libertad* arrived in San Francisco in 1854, 180 of the Chinese aboard (one out of every five) were dead from scurvy or ship's fever.

Some ships' captains were cruel and uncaring; yet others were more tolerant. Upon their arrival in San Francisco in 1852, the Chinese passengers of the *Balmoral* presented their captain with a magnificent silk flag as a token of their appreciation. It read: "Presented to J. B. Robertson by 464 of his Chinese passengers who have experienced much kindness and attention from him during the voyage from Kwangtung [Guangdong] to the Golden Hill."

"Every one of us found a friend in you" were the words inscribed on a pennant presented to Captain G. Chape of the British ship *Australia*. However, most immigrants endured a long and arduous passage to the country whose flag, because of its many stars, reminded them of flowers.

HOMESICKNESS

The words of a popular Cantonese folk song of the twentieth century reveal the deep homesickness most Chinese travelers felt as they began a new life so far from the land of their birth: "Drifting on a voyage of thousands of miles/I reached the Flowery Flag Nation to take my chances/sorrow is to be so far away from home."

When the immigrants first caught sight of the fog-shrouded hills near San Francisco, it reminded many of the land around the Pearl River Delta. Most Western travelers seeing the same

This view of San Francisco was many Chinese immigrants' first view of America in late nineteenth century. The foggy hills near the city, seen in the background, resembled the Pearl River Delta of their native land.

land described it as "raw, cold, and disagreeable." For the Chinese it looked much like home.

The chaotic scene at the docks in San Francisco during the 1850s and the 1860s must have reminded the immigrants of how far from China they really were. Sailors, agents of Chinese merchants, customs officials, and spectators all crowded around them on a pier covered with baskets, hats, matting, and bamboo poles. Amid the din of unrecognizable languages, they strained to hear the sound of a familiar dialect.

4

LIFE ACROSS THE PACIFIC

Somebody had brought to the pier large wagons for us. Out of the general babble, someone called out in our local dialect, and, like sheep recognizing the voice only, we blindly followed, and soon were piling into one of the waiting wagons. Everything was so strange and so exciting that my memory of the landing is just a big blur. The wagon made its way heavily over the cobblestones, turned some corners, ascended a steep climb, and stopped at a kind of clubhouse, where we spent the night. . . . As there were six of them, they were known as the "Six Companies." Newcomers were taken care of until relatives came to claim them and pay the bill.

—Huie Kin, recalling his arrival
in San Francisco in 1868.

This 1877 woodcut depicts the arrival of Chinese immigrants in San Francisco. After being inspected by customs officers, local Chinese merchants would greet the immigrants, house them, and provide them with jobs.

As immigrants like Huie Kin soon discovered, Chinese merchants had set up a complete support system. They were there to greet newcomers, house them, and, if necessary, provide them with jobs. These merchants also provided interpreters and community centers for these newly arrived immigrants. In many cases, some Chinese merchants loaned money to the prospective immigrant for passage across the Pacific. In China at that time, the merchant class did not have a high social status. But in the Chinese community in America, where there were no representatives of the scholar class or the ruling class, the merchant class assumed a leadership role.

Just as in China, travelers newly arrived in a city immediately sought out those who spoke the same dialect or were from the same clan. Also, as in China, *hui kuans* sprang up. After 800 Chinese arrived in San Francisco in 1849, the first merchants guild was organized. Gradually, as more and more immigrants arrived, a group of *hui kuans*, under the leadership of local merchants, assumed control of overseas Chinese society. The group was known as the Six Companies and served as, among other things, a mutual aid society.

MERCHANT AND SECRET SOCIETIES

The Six Companies were the unofficial spokesmen for the Chinese in San Francisco. They promoted the interests of the community and settled disputes between individuals and groups. For a time, they had their own police force. When lawyers were needed to defend Chinese rights, the Six Companies hired them. They also organized schooling for children, served as employment agencies, ran a hospital, and arranged for the return of the bones of deceased immigrants back to China.

The Six Companies had immense power over everyday life. When immigrants were ready to return to China, they needed clearance from the Six Companies. The Companies had an arrangement with the shipping companies that forbade anyone from buying a ticket back to China until all their debts had been paid.

Although the role of *hui kuans* like the Six Companies was more pronounced in America, the situation upon arrival in San Francisco would have been familiar to most immigrants.

How Others Saw Them

In his 1859 book, *The Tales of Peter Parley About Asia for Children*, Samuel Goodrich wrote: "The character of the Chinese is by no means an agreeable one. The men are servile, deceitful and utterly regardless of the truth. From the emperor to the beggar through every rank of society, through every grade of office, there is a system of cheating, and hypocrisy, practiced without remorse. . . . No faith whatever, can in general, be reposed in the Chinese."

Denis Kearney, an Irishman and leader of California's Workingmen's Party was a leading spokesman for the anti-Chinese movement: "Before you and before the world, we declare that the Chinaman must leave our shores. We declare that white men, and women, and boys, and girls, cannot live as the people of the great republic should and compete with the single Chinese coolie in the labor market. . . . Death is preferable to an American to life on a par with the Chinaman."

A witness speaking before the Joint Congressional Committee to Investigate Chinese Immigration in 1876 claimed "[The Chinese are] as inferior to any race God ever made . . . there are none so low. I believe that the Chinese have no souls to save, and if they have, they are not worth the saving."

Speaking out against anti-Chinese laws proposed in the United States Senate in 1879, Senator Hannibal Hamlin noted that the principles of human liberty and the rights of man were firmly rooted in the foundation of this country. Now, with the arrival of a few Chinese, he asked whether the tradition of America "as 'the home of the free,' where the outcast of every nation, where the child of every creed and of every clime would breathe our free air"—should now be reversed. "I am as indifferent to all the danger that shall come away down into the stillness of ages from the immigration of the Chinese. Treat them . . . like Christians, and they will become good American citizens."

Speaking against the Chinese Exclusion Act in 1882, Congressman Joyce said, "I would not vote for it if the time were reduced to one year or even one hour, because I believe that the total prohibition of these people from our shores for any length of time, however short, is not only unnecessary and uncalled for, but it is a cowardly repudiation, in our delight with a weak nation, of a just and long established principle in our government as well as a bold and open violation of the letter and spirit of our solemn treaty obligations with the people of China."

The Chinese merchant exchange in San Francisco, as depicted in an 1882 issue of *Harpers* magazine. Merchants became the unofficial spokesmen for the Chinese in San Francisco.

Almost immediately the Chinese found themselves immersed in family and clan relationships, while associating with people from the same region who spoke a familiar dialect. Within the various clan organizations were smaller organizations called *fongs,* where the relations were even closer. All this familiar Chinese culture greatly eased homesickness, but it also tended to separate immigrants from the developing American culture.

Secret societies, or *tongs*, also developed in San Francisco and other cities. Some were organized by immigrants who had been members of secret societies back in China. Others were set up by immigrants unable or unwilling to join regular family or district associations. Over time, some of these tongs became involved in illegal activities such as gambling, prostitution, and narcotics. Like criminal gangs today, disputes—called "tong wars"—sometimes erupted between rival tongs. However, the vast majority of immigrants arriving in San Francisco or Sacramento in the 1840s and 1850s had little contact with tongs.

Meanwhile, Chinese merchants quickly realized that a good living could be made by providing supplies for the tens of thousands of men flocking to California from all over the world. The diary entry of a Yankee miner read, "Were it not for the Chinese we might have starved the first year."

Meanwhile, the Chinese who went panning for gold found themselves in rough company. For the most part, the men who had made their way to California after 1849 were a ruthless bunch. The gold fields were a lawless place. Violence, drunkenness, and murders were common. Disputes were usually settled by brute force.

As it turned out, the patient Chinese were good at mining gold. They were so good, in fact, that it was claimed that, after they had worked a digging, there wouldn't be enough gold left to "fill the tooth of a bug." Part of the reason for that was that some of them had previously mined gold in China and other countries. They were also used to working together in groups—often a much more effective way to find gold than the every-man-for-himself methods favored by most white miners. As would happen so often in the years to come, the undisputed skills of the Chinese made them the target of racists. As one Yankee miner explained, those "little yellow men were hated by most of the white miners for their ability to grub out fortunes which they themselves had left—for greener pastures."

For white miners who had sacrificed everything to travel thousands of miles expecting a quick bonanza, the situation was a huge disappointment. Panning for gold was wet, hard work. For most, it was not profitable either. As early as the summer of 1849, it was said that only one man in a thousand made a living at it. Although gold was still being found, the price of food, supplies, and lodging was so great that any money made did not go far. In California, $140 would pay for the same amount of supplies as $25 in New York.

Another reason for the success of the Chinese was their familiarity with irrigation techniques long used in China. These came in handy because miners often needed to re-channel water to wash out gold-bearing gravel. When all the gold was gone from the rivers, the Chinese turned to hard rock or deep mining. When new machines and methods of digging were introduced to the mining business, the Chinese learned those, too. Unlike many white men, they were willing to work long hours for the big mining companies.

ANTI-CHINESE RIOTS

As is often the case with men whose dreams are dying, the frustrated whites looked for someone to take their anger out on. Their envy and self-pity was evident in a song of the day:

> We're working like a swarm of bees
> Scarcely making enough to live
> And two hundred thousand Chinese
> Are taking home the gold that
> We ought to have . . .

The first anti-Chinese riot occurred in 1849. Sixty Chinese were driven out of their camp by a band of angry miners. Such incidents occurred with increasing frequency

This nineteenth-century artwork depicts Chinese immigrants panning for gold in California. The Chinese, many of whom had prior experience mining gold in Asia, worked in groups and were noticeably skilled gold miners.

in the 1850s and 1860s, costing many Chinese their lives. After a while, instead of risking confrontations by competing with white miners for fresh claims, many Chinese instead took over abandoned claims that had supposedly been worked out. They knew there was often gold still left in those claims.

What happened to four Chinese miners near Round Trent, California, was typical. They'd paid a couple of hundred dollars for a "worthless" claim. After they'd mined $4,000 worth of gold in only two days, they were run off their claim by a mob of angry whites.

RAILROAD-BUILDING AND OTHER CHINESE CONTRIBUTIONS

Their mining experiences prepared Chinese workers well for building the western half of the Transcontinental Railroad. Already familiar with explosives and drilling tools, their knowledge proved invaluable to railway builders. "Wherever we put them, we found them good," said Charles Crocker, the railroad's general superintendent. "And they worked themselves into our favor to such an extent, we found if we were in a hurry for a job of work, it was better to put Chinese on it at once."

Many of the 13,000 Chinese who worked on the Transcontinental Railroad went on to other railway jobs. In fact, from Texas to Alaska, Chinese built all or part of almost every railroad line in the West. Although they provided the physical basis for the future industrial development of the West, their contributions have been largely ignored even though thousands of them died during the process.

Mining and railroads were far from the only lasting contributions that the Chinese made to the development of the West. In California, almost all the workers on farms and ranches were Chinese. By 1886, they made up almost 90 percent of the work force; the white men who had come to California were not interested in working on farms and ranches. If the Chinese had not been available, crops could not have been grown or harvested. Even as late as 1902, the *Los Angeles Times* declared that "the Chinese are the only people who will do ranch work faithfully."

But Chinese did more than just work on the ranches and farms. They used knowledge they brought from China to

The Chinese made major contributions to the fishing industry of San Francisco. Chinese immigrants also helped to develop California's first vineyards and reclaimed over a quarter-million acres of the San Joaquin and Sacramento valleys' wetlands for farming.

establish the raisin and fruit-growing industries. They helped to establish the first vineyards in California by picking the first grapes, and storing the first wines. They pioneered the fishing and canning industries along the West Coast from San Diego north to Alaska.

The Chinese also shaped the land itself. In the northern San Joaquin and Sacramento valleys, they reclaimed over a quarter-million acres of wetlands. Using techniques learned in China, they built thousands of miles of levees (embankments for preventing flooding), creating some of the richest farmland on earth. When they were finished, land that had been selling at $6 to $7 per acre was worth up to $100 an acre.

The present-day city of San Francisco was once another Chinese reclamation project. They built a six-mile-long sea wall and then, in an era before earth-moving machines were available, labored for years with shovels and carts to fill in the tidal flats behind it. The area they rescued from the sea is now the heart of the business and financial district—some of the highest-priced land in America! Everywhere they went, the Chinese added value to the land. As early as the 1870s, the former surveyor general of California estimated that—in less than three decades—Chinese workers had added at least $290 million dollars to the economy of the state.

Despite the fact that the Chinese contributed more to the building of the West than any other minority, they found themselves the targets of racism and discrimination. What made those attacks especially dangerous was the fact that they received no protection from the law. The supposed inferiority of the Chinese was upheld by the courts.

INJUSTICE TOWARD THE CHINESE

In 1853, a man named George W. Hall was convicted of murdering a Chinese man and sentenced to hang. His lawyer appealed the case to the California Supreme Court. Three Chinese had witnessed the murder and testified against Hall at the original trial. The law at the time held that no blacks or Indians could give testimony against a white man. The Supreme Court ruled that, since the Chinese were not white, they should not have been allowed to testify against a white man either. The court ordered that Hall be set free.

In the face of such legalized injustice, most Chinese had little choice but to work harder with the hope that they could soon save enough to return home to their families in China. Meanwhile, they did their best to keep a low profile. Many retreated to the relative safety of the Chinatowns in larger cities.

5

THE "YELLOW PERIL"

The anti-Chinese feelings that arose in the United States in the 1870s and 1880s were out of proportion to their numbers. Most Americans could go their entire lives without seeing a person of Chinese descent. Of the 50 million people living in the United States at the beginning of the 1880s, a mere 105,000 (or 0.2 percent) were Chinese.

The situation was a bit different west of the Rocky Mountains, however, where Chinese immigrants made up 5.8 percent of the population. Their labor on railroads, in mining, and in agriculture had contributed greatly to the economic development of the region. By the 1870s, more and more Chinese were working in factories where items such as shirts, shoes, boots, and cigars were made.

Up until the 1870s, there had been a labor shortage in America.

This political cartoon from the 1870s depicts a racist mob coming to attack a Chinese man, only to find him protected by Columbia, an American symbol of liberty. Chinese immigrants became victims of fear and racism when a weakened U.S. economy made white Americans and Chinese immigrants compete for the few available jobs.

During the Civil War in the 1860s, the army had needed so many soldiers that factories used all the workers they could find. A rapidly expanding economy after the war kept labor demand high. That all changed in the middle of the 1870s, when the country was hit with an economic depression. Suddenly, millions found themselves without jobs. Because the country was changing from an agriculturally based economy to an industrial economy, this was the nation's first experience with large-scale unemployment.

It was a huge shock, and few people understood the real reasons for unemployment. Unscrupulous politicians and newspaper editors soon realized they could attract support by drumming up feelings against those who "were taking away jobs that belonged to white men." No one ever accused the Chinese of being poor workers. In fact, the problem was just the opposite. As Lee Chew, a Chinese commenting on that period noted:

> It was the jealousy of laboring men of other nationalities—especially the Irish—that raised all the outcry against the Chinese. No one would hire an Irishman, German, Englishman or Italian when he could get a Chinese, because our countrymen [were] so much more honest, industrious, steady, sober, and painstaking. The Chinese were persecuted, not for their vices, but for their virtues.

Their performance as workers in the United States showed that, if they had been allowed to, Chinese would have become a valuable part of America's industrial working class. However, prejudice caused the American Federation of Labor (A.F.L.) unions to refuse Chinese membership. In fact, the A.F.L. was one of the strongest voices against the Chinese. Fear and jealousy among its members caused them to see the Chinese as a threat to their own well-being.

It was hard not to conclude that such anti-Chinese feelings stemmed from racist attitudes. Up to 800,000 Europeans were arriving in the United States every year. Most received citizenship and voting rights within a few years. Meanwhile, the few thousand Chinese arriving each year—out of the 380,000 residents of California in 1860, there were 33,000 Chinese—were denied citizenship and seen as the principal cause of white unemployment.

Of course, in an era before social security and unemployment insurance, being without a job was a desperate situation. At the height of the economic downturn in California, between 50,000 and 100,000 hungry men were without jobs. The widespread belief in "Manifest Destiny"—the idea that it was the divine mission of Christians to expand west and enlighten pagans, that is, non-Christians—contributed to the angry mood. The very presence of the Chinese—let alone that so many were skilled workers—made that notion seem questionable.

Many workers needed little encouragement to take out their anger and frustration on the Chinese. "We do not let the Indian stand in the way of civilization," said Horatio Seymour, a former governor of New York, "so why let the Chinese barbarian?" Seymour's belief that the Chinese were inferior beings was in the mainstream of public opinion during his day. It was even reflected in an entry in the *Encylopædia Britannica* from 1842, "A Chinaman is cold, cunning and distrustful; always ready to take advantage of those he has to deal with; extremely covetous and deceitful: quarrelsome, vindictive, but timid and dastardly."

On the West Coast, such attitudes caused the Chinese to become the preferred scapegoats for the country's labor problems. Once praised as hard-working, honest, and peaceful, they now found themselves described as dangerous, dirty, and deceitful. In California, an Irishman named Denis Kearney helped form the Workingmen's Party in 1877. In fiery speeches before huge crowds, Kearney accused the Chinese of stealing jobs from white men. His solution was to drive all Chinese from the United States. Kearney's speeches always ended with "The Chinese must go! They are stealing our jobs!"

Kearney's intolerant message made sense to desperate men who wanted to do *something* to better their situation. It provided a simple solution to a complex problem. His followers organized anti-Chinese organizations and held mass meetings to fight the "Yellow Peril," as they negatively dubbed Chinese laborers. Meanwhile, newspaper editors and political cartoonists, who believed that all Asians were inferior, attacked and ridiculed the Chinese in print. A typical cartoon showed rats escaping from a sinking ship. As they crawled ashore, they evolved into Chinese. Politicians warned that if the Chinese "invasion" were not stopped, it might well lead to the ruin of America.

ANTI-CHINESE VIOLENCE

Unable to vote for politicians who were sympathetic to their cause and denied the right to even testify in court, the Chinese increasingly found themselves the targets of violence. In 1871, hundreds were driven from their homes in Los Angeles in riots that killed 22 Chinese. Similar riots occurred all over the West during the next two decades. Chinese were forced to pay special taxes that no other group had to pay. Other laws forbade Chinese to farm, own land, join a union, or work for the state. Even employers who wanted to hire Chinese no longer dared to do so.

In 1877, rioters roamed San Francisco's Chinatown on three successive nights, beating any Chinese they could find and setting fire to Chinese businesses. It took army troops and some 5,000 citizen vigilantes to finally stop the violence—but not until a half-million dollars worth of damage was done.

ANTI-CHINESE POLITICAL MANEUVERS

Up until 1876, the "problem" of Chinese immigration had been mostly a local issue in California. The 1876 presidential election between Rutherford B. Hayes and Samuel J. Tilden, however, was the closest in history—Hayes won by one electoral vote. Because the Republican and Democrat parties were almost evenly balanced, it became obvious that California's votes could be very important in future elections. In an effort to win those votes, politicians of both parties began portraying the Chinese "problem" as a national emergency. Commenting on the "Chinese invasion" in 1879, President Hayes signaled where he stood on the issue: "Our experience in dealing with the weaker races—the Negroes and Indians . . . —is not encouraging . . . I would consider with favor any suitable measures to discourage the Chinese from coming to our shores."

In California, the anti-Chinese movement gathered momentum in 1879 when California drew up its second Constitution. Under the new Constitution's provisions, it was unlawful for either companies or state government to hire Chinese (not until the 1940s would it be legal for Chinese to work for the state). A year later, the governor declared March 4, 1880 a legal holiday for anti-Chinese demonstrations.

With the enthusiastic backing of California legislators, the United States Congress passed the Chinese Exclusion Act in 1882. For the first time in history an entire ethnic group was barred from immigrating to the United States. The act banned the entry of skilled and unskilled workers from China for ten years and denied them the right to become U.S. citizens. The law was extended and strengthened often, remaining in effect for the next 61 years. Although exemptions were made for merchants, students, teachers, and government officials, few Chinese emigrants fit those categories.

If the abolishment of slavery after the Civil War was a great step forward for racial equality in America, then the Exclusion Act was a huge step backward. Fearing for their lives and seeing no future here, some Chinese fled to other countries or back to China. Others—those unable to afford passage back to China or unwilling to return home in defeat—retreated to larger cities. "We were simply terrified," recalled Huie Kin of San Francisco's Chinatown in the 1870s and 1880s. "We kept indoors after dark for fear of being shot in the back. Children spit upon us as we passed by and called us rats." The passage of laws like the Exclusion Act encouraged those who felt like "clearing out the Chinese" from their towns.

When it became obvious that the Exclusion Act was going to pass in Congress, there was a final rush of Chinese to enter the United States before the doors closed (39,549 came in 1882). Even with that influx, so many immigrants had given up and returned to China or gone elsewhere that by 1883 the number of Chinese in the country had fallen by more than 12,000.

ANTI-CHINESE RIOTS AND MURDER

From the 1870s into the 1890s, Chinese living west of the Rocky Mountains were repeatedly terrorized by gangs of thugs. When a white man was killed during a police raid in Los Angeles' Chinatown, the city erupted. A huge mob destroyed Chinese houses and businesses and killed 22 Chinese, including women and children. One of the worst incidents occurred in Wyoming in 1885. During a night of violence, 11 Chinese living in the town of Rock Springs were burned alive in their cabins (17 others were murdered with rifles and other weapons). At Douglas Bar, Oregon, in the same year, 32 Chinese miners were murdered in their homes. Although the government of China demanded an investigation, the three men charged with the murders were eventually acquitted. In the racist atmosphere of the time, it was very unusual for a white man to be found guilty of a crime against a Chinese.

One of the larger riots occurred in Seattle in 1886 when an anti-Chinese committee demanded that all Chinese leave the area. Along with the chief of police and the entire police force, they led a group of wagons into Seattle's Chinatown. The committee forced the Chinese there to pack their belongings and then drove them to the docks, where they were to be loaded onto a steamship bound for San Francisco. Some sympathetic white citizens attempted to stop what was going on by organizing a "Home Guard." The rioting that ensued killed several people and forced President Cleveland to call in the National Guard. It was months before the city finally calmed down.

In nearby Tacoma, Washington, 3,000 Chinese were given 24 hours to leave town. Angry mobs were evicting Chinese from towns all over the West. In an attempt to escape the violence, many Chinese fled to other parts of the United States. By 1890, there were Chinese in almost every state in the union.

Chinese workers flee attacking mobs in an 1885 massacre in Rock Springs, Wyoming. Out of the 28 Chinese murdered in the massacre, 11 were burned alive. In the 1870s, a period of heightened terrorism began against Chinese living west of the Rocky Mountains that would last over two decades.

Forced to live in larger towns for safety, Chinese immigrants in the West found their world shrinking. Many risked death if they strayed beyond the borders of Chinatown. Like most American men, the Chinese had not brought along their wives when they came to California. In those days, no respectable woman—American or Chinese—would think of going to such a place alone. Being forced to live in a bachelor society mostly devoid of women and children was a lonely and cruel existence for men from a society in which family ties were the foundation of the entire culture.

DISCRIMINATION IN SCHOOLS

Although there were very few Chinese families in America, even they did not escape the hand of discrimination. By law, Chinese children were banned from going to white schools. When Mamie Tape, the daughter of Mary and Joseph Tape, was not allowed to attend public school in San Francisco, her parents decided to fight. They sued the San Francisco Board of Education. They argued their case so convincingly that they actually won. The court even affirmed the right of Chinese children to public education. The victory, however, was short-lived. As school boards would also do in the South—Mississippi and Louisiana, for example—the San Francisco school board got around the law by creating "separate but equal" segregated school systems that lasted for more than 60 years.

CHINESE LOOK TO BUSINESSES

Discouraged or intimidated from working with whites or in businesses in direct competition with white businesses, many Chinese looked for ways of making a living where they could be completely independent. One of the best options they found was running a laundry. Although it was hot and hard work, it took very little money to start and white men would never think of doing such "women's work." Owning a laundry was considered a good business because it took only four or five years to earn enough money for a trip home to China. Also, those who owned their own businesses could save money by sleeping on the premises.

Owning a small business or restaurant was another popular option. Like operating a laundry, it meant endless hours of work, but at least a man could be his own boss. Other Chinese with cooking or gardening skills were hired by the wealthy as domestic help. Since most Americans had little actual contact with the Chinese, misinformation about them was still widespread.

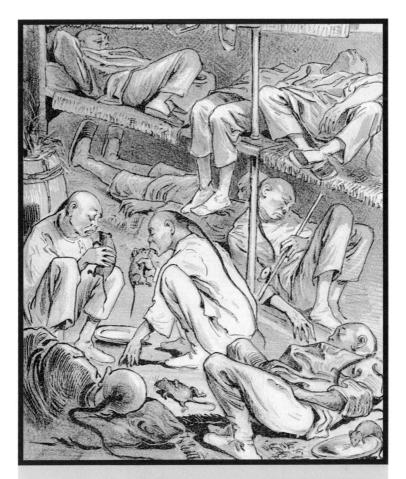

A political cartoon from the late nineteenth century perpetuates the myth that Chinese immigrants would work for such low wages that they had to eat rats and live in squalor.

MYTHS ABOUT THE CHINESE

One of the most common misconceptions was the coolie myth. Critics of the Chinese in America contended that they had come to this country as virtual slaves—like those who had been shanghaied and sent to South America or the Caribbean. It was claimed they would work for wages so low that white workers could not compete. In truth, virtually all the Chinese workers who came to America either paid their own way or borrowed money for the passage. They were here because they wanted to be, and they were no more slaves than the Europeans who came to this country as indentured servants.

"Hair and Air" Laws

During the height of anti-Chinese sentiment in California during the 1870s and 1880s, San Franciscan politicians realized they could blame Chinese for the state's economic problems. Since they wanted the votes of the working man (and the Chinese could not vote), politicians began passing laws designed specifically to harass and humiliate the Chinese. Among these unfair laws (all were eventually declared unconstitutional) were:

The Sidewalk Ordinance of 1870

This law prohibited people who used poles to carry merchandise from walking on the sidewalk. Since all non-Chinese used wagons or carts to carry their loads, it was obvious toward whom the law was directed.

The Cubic Air Ordinance of 1871

In the 1870s, San Francisco's Chinatown consisted of seven square blocks. Because it was unsafe for Chinese to live outside it, there was severe over-crowding. This law requiring 500 cubic feet of living space for each adult led to the arrest of hundreds of Chinese. It was finally repealed after jails became so crowded that critics pointed out that by imprisoning so many in tight quarters, the government was breaking the same law it was enforcing.

The Queue Ordinance of 1873

Under the law in China, men were required to comb their hair into single long braids called queues. Since most Chinese hoped to return to China, they kept their hair as required. The queue law forced all prisoners to have their hair cut so that it was not more than one inch long. Having their hair cut against their will was a particularly humiliating experience.

The Laundry Ordinance of 1873

The law required anyone who carried laundry without using a horse-drawn wagon to pay a high tax. Its obvious intent was to drive all Chinese, who used poles to transport laundry, out of the laundry business, but it did not succeed.

Another myth was that the Chinese were carriers of filth and disease. That had more to do with the close quarters they were forced to live in after the anti-Chinese riots of the 1870s and 1880s than any personal habits. In fact, when Chinese workers first arrived in the gold fields of California, their cleanliness amazed the European immigrants with whom they came in contact. At a time when few men even bothered with their Saturday night bath, Chinese workers bathed after work every day.

The Chinese were also accused of being opium addicts. There was some truth to that allegation—although few critics bothered to mention that it was the European nations who had introduced opium into China against its will. Some Chinese in America, particularly depressed and discouraged men lonely for their families, filled the emptiness of the little spare time they had by smoking opium. However, its usage was never as widespread as its critics claimed it was.

RECREATION AND CULTURAL ACTIVITIES

Gambling was popular recreation for the Chinese. Its appeal was that there was always a chance to win a fortune and be able to leave behind the unwelcome circumstances of the present. Playing the lottery and a card game called *fantan* were some of the ways men gambled. There were other more wholesome forms of recreation. One of the most popular was the Chinese theater. The first Chinese play in America was presented in San Francisco in 1853. By 1879, a three-story Chinese theater with a capacity of 2,500 people had been built in Chinatown. For decades, audiences of mostly Chinese men sat watching the plays and listening to the Chinese orchestra while smoking cigars or cigarettes and eating mandarin oranges. The long historical dramas and the actors' dazzling costumes helped the audience lose themselves in an imaginary world that reminded them of the country they had once lived in.

Curious Americans look on as Chinese men bow before altars in a joss house (or Chinese temple) in San Francisco in the early 1870s. In addition to religion, Chinese honored their heritage by celebrating traditional Chinese holidays and engaging in traditional Chinese forms of entertainment.

The Chinese found other ways to keep their culture alive. They built altars, called joss houses, to honor their gods. Usually such altars were located in the top stories of buildings to guard against the idols being stolen by thieves and to ensure that nothing used by human hands came above the gods. They celebrated the New Year with lion dances and firecrackers. Special care was taken to celebrate traditional

Chinese holidays at the appropriate time of year. Tung Pok Chin recalled New Year's celebrations in his childhood village in Guangdong Province:

> From behind the bamboo thickets we lured the dragon to our hideaway, teasing and taunting it along. "Dragon! Dragon! This way!" we took turns shouting. Dazed and confused, it danced toward each child who called to it. Then, just when it was exactly where we wished it to be, we lit the firecrackers and threw them toward the dragon from all directions. It jumped, pounced, and rolled over in the dirt roads of the back country as we pursued it. We surrounded it again, shouting from all sides as before, burning away the evil spirits of the old year with our fireworks, until the dragon dies and rose anew with all of its power and glory. . . .

As Chin's memory of New Year's confirms, despite all the persecution they faced, most Chinese found ways of maintaining ties to the land of their birth.

6

THE TIDE TURNS

Well, I took the advice of the young fellows and I got myself a dictionary. I think I carried that dictionary for about three to four years, in the back of my pocket. . . . I walk on the street and I see a word and I bring out my dictionary and I find out what that word means. So when I learn one word and two and three, in time I build my own sentences. . . . If you accumulate words like the way you put money in the bank, two words in your notebook a day, 365 days a year, you will learn over seven hundred words in one year. From seven hundred words, that's all you need to get around; and from seven hundred words you can build thousands of sentences. And this is how I did it.

—*Immigrant Arthur Wong on how he learned English despite not having the money or time for English lessons*

B y law, the Chinese Exclusion Act was due to expire in 1892. However, it would be extended and modified for more than 60 years. With each extension, more restrictions to "plug loopholes" were placed on Chinese immigration. Not until World War II was the law repealed permanently.

LEGAL HARASSMENT

In 1888, six years after the first Exclusion Act became law, Congress passed the Scott Act. A particularly cruel piece of legislation, it canceled the right of Chinese immigrants visiting abroad to return home to America. Twenty-thousand immigrants

The Angel Island detention center in San Francisco Bay was known for the cruel procedures immigration officers practiced, particularly against Chinese immigrants. After undergoing long interrogations and humiliating medical examinations, a Chinese immigrant could still be detained at Angel Island for months, or even years.

were away visiting relatives in China at the time of its passage. Even though they had authentic re-entry permits, neither they nor the 600 or so who were aboard ships coming back to America allowed to re-enter the country. Enforcement of the law broke up many families and further isolated the Chinese remaining in the United States.

Ironically, only two years before, the government of France had presented the United States with a huge statue to be placed on an island in New York Harbor. The Statue of Liberty was supposed to be a beacon of liberty to the rest of the world. Its base bears the famous words: "Give me your tired, your poor/Your huddled masses yearning to breathe free." The Scott Act and similar anti-Chinese legislation made it clear that some Americans believed those words should not apply to the Chinese.

When Congress extended the Exclusion Act in 1892, it included a new provision requiring all Chinese aliens to carry a certificate of identity. Anyone found without a certificate could be arrested and deported without trial. Not until Nazi Germany a half-century later would a government require a people to carry identity cards.

The Chinese did not endure such outrages passively. The Six Companies hired lawyers and fought back as best they could. In 1898, they even succeeded in getting the U.S. Supreme Court to rule that Chinese Americans born in this country were entitled to constitutional protection and could not be treated differently from other citizens.

Still, the legal and physical harassment continued. San Francisco's Chinatown was blockaded in 1900 because of fears that it was a source of the plague. Similar fears led to Honolulu's Chinatown being completely burned down in a so-called "sanitary fire." Meanwhile, racist politicians had been appointed to enforce immigration laws. Their goal was to prevent new Chinese immigration and get rid of ethnic Chinese already living in the United States. In the 12 months after June of

1904, over 1,400 Chinese were arrested and 647 deported merely on the suspicion that they might not have entered lawfully.

The treatment of Chinese Americans grew so bad that a boycott of American goods was organized in China in 1905. In two years, U.S. trade with China dropped from $57 million to $26 million. The boycott did not end the racist treatment, but it drew nationwide attention to the brutality and unfairness of the men who ran the immigration system. President Roosevelt was forced to replace some of the worst officials.

Still, the harsh immigration laws gave Chinese who missed their families no choice but to smuggle their own wives, children, and kinsmen into this country. The "slot racket" was one name for a system they invented to help each other out. When a Chinese U.S. citizen returned from a visit to China, he or she would report the birth of a son or daughter there. Children of U.S. citizens automatically become citizens, so this created a "slot" someone (often from a different family) could later use to bring in a child. Catching these illegal "paper sons and daughters" soon became the main preoccupation of the immigration authorities.

It was a job that became much harder for officials after the great San Francisco earthquake and fire of 1906. The disaster destroyed most city records. Many Chinese took the opportunity to claim that they were U.S. citizens born in San Francisco. Since it was impossible to check whether their claims were true, many became citizens this way. Immigration authorities, however, were not happy about what was happening.

DETENTION AT ANGEL ISLAND

After 1910 all immigrants to the West Coast were sent to a small island in San Francisco Bay soon after their arrival in San Francisco. Except for the Chinese immigrants, all other nationalities were released after a few hours. Angel Island was notorious for its harsh treatment. Its purpose was not so much to process immigrants as to discourage them. It was assumed that almost all

Chinese lied to gain entry to the United States. Presumed guilty of fraud, the immigrants had to prove their innocence while being held in a jail-like setting for as long as two or three years.

Examinations and interrogations usually lasted two or three days, but the waiting could go on for months. Those who failed were sent back to China. In some years, the rejection rate was as high as 85 percent. To prepare for the nerve-wracking ordeal, paper sons and daughters studied and memorized all the information they could on their new "families." Worse than the tests for many were the physical examinations, which were made as humiliating as possible. Immigrants had to take off all their clothes and stand naked in front of each other while waiting for a doctor to examine them for diseases.

After the physical exams, men were marched to one set of barracks; women to another. Each barrack was just a large, bare room with rows of bunks. Men and women ate at separate times so they could not meet and talk with one another while waiting out their detention. There was even a windowless cell used for solitary confinement of inmates who became upset by being imprisoned for so long. Although they could see the city of San Francisco through the bars of their windows, some immigrants were so miserable about being cut off from their families that they committed suicide.

Others expressed their misery by carving poems like this on the barracks walls:

> Why do I have to sit in jail?
> It is only because my country is weak and my family is poor.
> My parents wait at the door in vain for news;
> My wife and child wrap themselves in their quilt,
> Sighing with loneliness.
> Even should I be allowed to enter this country,
> When can I make enough to return to China with wealth?

The conditions on Angel Island were so miserable that, in 1922 when the Commissioner General of Immigration visited, he declared the buildings filthy firetraps unfit for human habitation. Even his recommendations were ignored. Angel Island continued to be used until 1940 when the administration building finally burned down.

DROP IN CHINESE IMMIGRATION

Around the time of the Commissioner General's 1922 visit, the number of Chinese immigrants in America had dropped to an all-time low. From a high of 107,000 in 1880, the total number in the Chinese–American community had shrunk to 61,000.

Most of these were men—in 1910 the ratio of males to females was 26 to 1. However, a small influx of women after the 1906 earthquake meant that a few more Chinese men were able to get married and begin raising families. That may have led the anti-Chinese forces in Congress to pass the last major exclusion law.

CONGRESS STOPS IMMIGRATION

The Immigration Act of 1924 made it illegal for native-born U.S. citizens to bring their China-born wives and children to America. The law was a devastating blow for men who had been working hard, sometimes for decades, to save enough money to bring their families to the United States. Any hope that they could now make a real home in this country seemed gone. During the next five years, not one Chinese woman emigrated from China to California.

Such cruelty was becoming harder for fair-minded Americans to tolerate. In hearings before Congress, the head of the Chinese–American Citizens' Alliance testified about the hardships that the law imposed on loyal American citizens who could not be with their wives. He was supported by California Congresswoman Florence Kahn, who pleaded that "something may be done to remedy the deplorable situation in which this group of intelligent, patriotic, native-born American citizens find themselves. They are deprived by law of one of the fundamental rights of the human race, namely, the right to enjoy family life."

WAR MAKES ALLIES OF CHINA AND AMERICA

Perhaps swayed by such testimony, in 1930 Congress changed the 1924 law to allow the admission of Chinese wives who had married U.S. citizens before 1924. The repeal contributed to the continuing growth of Chinese–American families. It was not until World War II that harassment of Chinese by immigration authorities began coming to an end. After the attack on Pearl Harbor on December 7, 1941, there was little doubt that Japan was America's mortal enemy.

China, too, had been attacked by Japan. In the days following Pearl Harbor, both the United States and the Republic of China declared war on Japan. Suddenly, the two countries had a common enemy. The Chinese in America responded enthusiastically to the call to arms. It allowed them to express their patriotism for the United States while helping defend the country where their relatives still lived.

This open letter, entitled "A Memo to Mr. Hitler, Horohito & Co.," appeared in the newspaper read by the San Francisco Chinese community:

> Have you heard the bad news? America is out to get you. America has a grim but enthusiastic bombing party started and you're the target in the parlor game.
>
> San Francisco Chinatown, U.S.A., is joining the party. Chinatown will have fun blasting you to hell. Chinatown is proud to be a part of Freedom's legion in freeing all the decent people of the world . . .

The memo ended with this postscript: "More bad news. Everyone in Chinatown is going to this party. We're NOT missing this one." That attitude was reflected in the numbers of Chinese who served in the armed forces. Almost one out of every four Chinese males (13,499) either enlisted or was

This man is your **FRIEND**

Chinese

He fights for **FREEDOM**

A U.S. government poster from World War II reflects the active role Chinese Americans took in the war effort. Approximately a quarter of Chinese-American males fought in World War II.

drafted into the war effort.

"To men of my generation," said Charlie Leong of San Francisco, "World War II was the most important historic event of our times. For the first time we felt we could make it in American society."

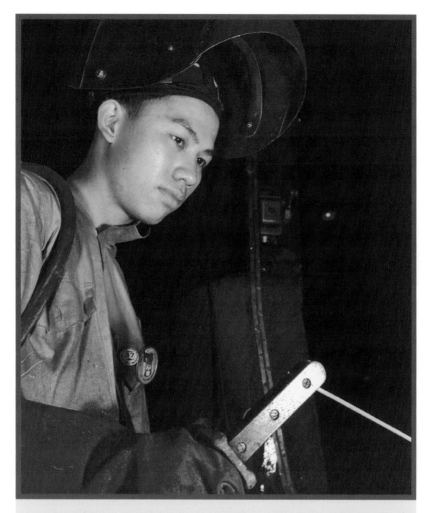

A Chinese-American boatyard worker welds a steel ramp boat for the war in 1942. World War II marked the beginning of widespread acceptance for Chinese Americans that culminated in the repeal of the Chinese Exclusion Act.

Harold Liu of New York felt that, for the first time, other Americans accepted Chinese as friends. "It was just a whole different era and in the community we began to feel very good about ourselves," he recalled. "My own brothers went into the service. We were so proud that they were in uniform."

After decades of stereotyping, newspapers and magazines began describing Chinese as polite, moderate, and hard-working. Meanwhile, thousands of Chinese—both men and women—found jobs in the defense industry. Accepted into worlds that had once been closed to them, their confidence grew.

CHINESE IMMIGRATION RE-OPENS

By 1943 it was becoming increasingly obvious that it made little sense for Chinese Americans to be fighting for freedom and democracy overseas while they were denied equality at home. Speaking in support of a bill to repeal the Chinese Exclusion Act, President Roosevelt said, "In the effort to carry out the policy of excluding Chinese laborers—Chinese coolies—grave injustice and wrong have been done by the nation to the people of China and, therefore, ultimately to this nation itself."

Roosevelt's recommendation was accepted and, after almost 100 years, Chinese immigration was opened up again. The law also permitted immigrants to become naturalized citizens. Although it was more symbolic than substantive—only 105 immigrants a year were allowed in—the law marked a major turning point in attitudes toward Chinese Americans.

Another turning point came two years after the war ended. A 1947 amendment to the 1945 War Brides Act allowed Chinese Americans to end long years of separation from their wives by bringing them to America. They were also allowed to return to China to marry and bring their brides to the United States. This law gave an unprecedented number of Chinese women a chance to enter the country. It helped produce a new generation of native-born Chinese. For the first time ever, Chinese Americans began establishing families at a rate similar to that of other Americans.

Like other Americans, returning Chinese servicemen used the GI Bill of Rights to help pay for a college education or make

The Plant Wizard

Lue Gim Gong was barely a teenager when he arrived in San Francisco from his native Canton, China. Then, at the age of 16, he headed east to work in a shoe factory in North Adams, Massachusetts. There, while learning English at a church Sunday school, he met Fanny Burlingame. Her uncle had been an ambassador to China, and she was able to speak to Lue in Chinese. Fearing for his health (he was a very frail boy), Fanny arranged for Lue to work in her family's nursery. He converted to Christianity and lived with the Burlingames until 1877.

When he caught tuberculosis, Lue returned to China, hoping that the warmer climate would be good for his health. But because of his religious conversion, he was not accepted in China. He returned to the United States and lived on an orchard Fanny had purchased in De Land, Florida. During Lue's first winter in Florida, a severe freeze had destroyed most of the orange crop. Lue began conducting experiments to develop an orange that would resist cold.

By cross-pollinating two different kinds of oranges, Lue developed a new kind of orange that was large and full of juice and could endure cold weather with little damage. It also could hang on trees during the rainy summers. The "Lue Gim Gong Orange" would become the basis for the entire citrus industry in Florida. In 1911, Lue was awarded the Wilder Silver Medal by the American Pomological Society for his new orange.

Continuing his experiments, Lue developed many unusual plants, including a rose bush that put forth 17 different varieties in seven different colors from a single root. He created a grapefruit that, although too woody to eat, could fill an entire room with a clean, sweet odor when cut. Among his other creations were peaches that ripened in time for Thanksgiving, sweet apples, and salmon-pink-colored raspberries.

Lue never profited greatly from his developments, and he lived alone with his two horses and his plants during his last years. He died in 1925, but there is a memorial to him in De Land, Florida. It includes a pavilion and life-size statue of Lue as he looked in 1890. Inscribed nearby are the words that guided his life, "No one should live in this world for himself alone, but to do good for those who come after him."

Chinese war brides attend Chinese-language Sunday school at Warminster Presbyterian Church in Minneapolis in 1950. The 1947 amendment to the 1945 War Brides Act allowed Chinese-American men to bring their wives from China into America.

payments on houses outside of Chinatown. No longer were their options for the future reduced to owning a small business or working in a laundry or restaurant.

Events in China after the war also had an effect on the changing attitudes toward Chinese Americans. A war broke out between the Communists and the Nationalists. America supported the Nationalists, but they lost the war and set up a government on the island of Taiwan. In 1949, Congress began allowing Chinese refugees from the losing side to enter the United States. However, with Communist governments in power in Russia and China, there was a widespread belief that another war could break out at any time. In the 1940s and 1950s, the so-called Cold War increased suspicion in America of anyone who looked "foreign." J. Edgar Hoover, head of the FBI, warned that any Chinese immigrant was a potential spy.

BLENDING INTO AMERICAN SOCIETY

Still, for most Chinese, those decades were a time of blending into society and adapting to new opportunities. By 1950, Chinese Americans lived almost exclusively in urban areas, and some were moving out of Chinatowns to previously all-white areas of cities. Others were joining the middle class for the first time. In the ten years preceding 1950, the numbers of Chinese in technical and professional jobs tripled. Jobs in fields such as medicine, dentistry, optometry, and pharmacy were particularly attractive because they offered both prestige and a degree of independence.

Scholars have long held high status in China; so, as Chinese-American families began growing and the children entered schools, traditional attitudes served them well. Given a fair chance, most Chinese children scored high marks in school.

Families began adopting American traditions like celebrating the Fourth of July and Thanksgiving, while keeping ancient Chinese traditions like the celebration of Chinese New Year and visiting the graves of ancestors in the spring and fall. Parents who feared their children would forget the old ways sent their children to special language schools to learn how to speak and write Chinese.

Still, because society was so much more open toward Chinese-American children born in the 1940s and 1950s than it had been toward their parents, many were beginning to see themselves as more American than Chinese. After nearly 100 years of an often precarious existence, the Chinese community in America was at last beginning to put down deeper roots.

7 INTO THE MELTING POT:
The Chinese–American Influence

In the summer of 1959, we moved out of Chinatown.

Just seven years before, the restrictions barring people of minority races from owning property in various parts of Oakland had been lifted, and the Chinese of Oakland had fanned out. This marked another of the differences between the Chinatowns of Oakland and San Francisco. Across the bridge in Dai Fow [San Francisco], Chinatown was its own state, a community so defined and powerful, so protective of its citizens that they often found it both unnecessary and difficult to leave. In Oakland, people who lived in Chinatown were anxious to get out. Sure, they felt welcome and comfortable there, but, like Oakland itself, it was lifeless compared to San Francisco. As soon as they were allowed to, and could afford to move to another neighborhood, they packed up.

—Ben Fong-Torres

Chinese Americans shop for oranges at a market in San Francisco's Chinatown in preparation for a New Year's feast. San Francisco has one of the largest concentrations of Chinese Americans in the United States.

Up until 1960, there never had been more than 200,000 Chinese on the mainland of the United States. In the ten years between 1960 and 1970, the population nearly doubled, going from 237,000 to 436,000. At the same time, the civil rights movement of the 1960s was changing the way Americans thought about minorities. During the middle of that decade, Chinese immigration got a big boost when a Congress more tolerant of minorities passed the Immigration and Nationality Act. This 1965 law changed the number of

Chinese immigrants each year. Instead of 105 individuals, now up to 20,000 could be admitted to the United States. In 1990, the law was modified to encourage the immigration of professional people or those with exceptional scientific or artistic ability.

CHINESE–AMERICAN POPULATION TODAY

This opened the doors for a huge increase in Chinese immigration. The Chinese who came after 1968 were different from those who had come before (the law did not actually go into effect until July 1 of that year). They tended to be more educated and to come from parts of China other than the area around Canton. Many spoke an entirely different dialect called Mandarin.

The new arrivals were not always content to live in the cramped quarters of a big-city Chinatown. Because they had professional and technical skills, many made their homes in other parts of the city or even the suburbs. A key part of the 1965 law directed that immigration give preference to relatives of Chinese who had become U.S. citizens. There was a minimum five-year waiting period to become a U.S. citizen. Each time an immigrant became a naturalized citizen, another group of his or her relatives back in China became eligible to follow the relative to the United States.

Many Chinese took advantage of the opportunity of citizenship privileges. This kind of chain migration has accounted for most of the new Chinese arrivals in the United States since 1968. There has been a remarkable increase since then. By the time the 2000 census was taken, Chinese Americans, with a population of 2.4 million, had become the largest Asian ethnic group in this country. Except for Texas and Hawaii, Chinese tend to live on the east or west coasts. The five states with the largest numbers of Chinese Americans are California, New York, Texas, New Jersey, and Massachusetts. Hawaii contains the highest percentage of

Chinese Americans of any state. The largest concentrations of Chinese are in Chinatowns in places such as San Francisco, New York City, Boston, and Honolulu.

Because so many Chinese immigrated to the United States in the last several decades, most Chinese in this country today were born somewhere else. That was not the case before 1960. Since so many present-day Chinese Americans grew up overseas they have been forced to learn American ways quickly—not always an easy adjustment. Still, by most standards, Chinese Americans are doing well in America.

INCOME

In 1990, the average family income for Chinese Americans was $4,000 to $5,000 higher than for white families. In addition, they were almost twice as likely to have better-paying professional, managerial, or technical jobs. So many Chinese-American students excel in school that, as a group, their grades are higher than Euro-Americans. They also tend to go on to college in greater numbers. Although accounting for only 3 percent of the U.S. population in 1995, Chinese Americans made up 5 percent of the college population.

After decades of being labeled a danger to America, Chinese Americans are no longer described as the "Yellow Peril." No longer called "uncivilized heathens incapable of fitting into proper society," they are hailed for their achievements. Because of their considerable educational and economic attainments, as well as their relatively low rates of divorce and delinquency, politicians and the media praise them as a "model minority."

However, the tendency for society to see the Chinese in simplistic terms—either Yellow Peril or model minority—is not very helpful. Such labels make it harder to see that the situation is much more complex. For example, while it is true that Chinese-Americans' average income is up to $5,000 more than white families, it is rarely mentioned that they tend to live in states where the cost of living is also much higher. They also average more persons working per family than whites. In many cases, their greater incomes are due to having more people working rather than actual higher incomes per person.

SPLITS AMONG CHINESE AMERICANS

It is also rarely mentioned that, while many educated Chinese immigrants are doing very well, those without strong educational backgrounds or the ability to speak English struggle in low-paying jobs. In 1990, 16 percent of the immigrants from mainland China had less than a fifth-grade education. Unable to speak English well, and with few marketable skills, these immigrants are often "ghetto-ized." Unable to get good jobs, they have been forced to live in poor housing with others in the same situation.

Wealth

The situation of diverse wealth has led to a split between "uptown" and "downtown" Chinese. Like other ethnic groups, the wealthy and the poor do not always get along well. Other splits in the Chinese community exist between the Cantonese who emigrated from Guangdong Province (90–95 percent of all immigrants before 1965) and the more recent immigrants from Hong Kong, Taiwan, or more northern parts of mainland China.

Traditions

Children of first-generation immigrants have experienced another kind of split. Torn between the traditional Chinese values of being loyal to their families and determination to make their own way in a new society, they have had to figure out exactly what it means to be Chinese American.

Some Chinese-American children reject Chinese values completely. Striving to be as much like white Americans as possible, they are sometimes called "bananas"—yellow on the outside, white on the inside. Most, however, have tried to find

Festival participants perform a lion dance in Boston's Chinatown. Lion and dragon dances are a well-known part of Chinese New Year celebrations.

some way to maintain good relations with their parents, yet blend into the multicultural society they must live in.

Although Ben Fong-Torres eventually became a writer for *Rolling Stone* magazine, his childhood was typical. His family owned a restaurant in Oakland, California, and he and his brothers and sisters were expected to spend all of their spare time helping out. "The time for socializing would be after graduation—from *college* that is," he recalled. "I owed it to the family to be at the restaurant. 'That's how it is with Chinese,' my parents said."

Language

Like many first-generation Chinese, Fong-Torres' parents felt little need to learn English to survive. After all, they were making a living without it. Their children, however, could see that they would have to learn English if they wanted to succeed in school and later in life. On the other hand, they felt little compulsion to speak proper Chinese, even if it was the language of their parents. The language barrier that developed between Fong-Torres' parents and their children was repeated in many families. It contributed to a split between the generations that was greatly troubling to the older generation.

PARACHUTE KIDS

A recent phenomenon is the so-called "parachute kids." Also known as *xia liu xue sheng* or "little overseas students," parachute kids are students, mostly from Taiwan and Hong Kong, who come to live in the United States without their parents. These are not college students but children of junior high age or younger. They live either with distant relatives or with paid caretakers, although some simply stay alone in a house or apartment their parents arrange for them to live in. Parachute kids and their parents are willing to make great sacrifices in the hope that they will get a better education in America.

FOOD

The Chinese have taken advantage of the opportunities that America has presented them despite all the obstacles placed in their path. In the process, they and those who came before them have enriched society in countless ways. Food is perhaps the most recognizable Chinese contribution to American culture. Over thousands of years, the Chinese learned how to combine spices, flavors, and textures to make tasty and nutritious meals. In China, the preparation of food is considered an art, not a chore. As far back as the California Gold Rush, Chinese cooks were making meals for miners who, up to then, subsisted on a diet of mostly meat and beans. Often the miners had no idea what they were eating, but in most cases they had to admit it tasted good. One hundred fifty years later, there are Chinese restaurants on every corner of America.

CHINESE HEALTH TRADITIONS

Health and medicine are two other areas in which Chinese traditions have made a successful transition to America. Chinese systems of movement and exercise like *tai chi* are becoming increasingly recommended as ways to maintain physical and mental health. The ancient Chinese practice of acupuncture (which involves placing needles in various parts of the body) has been shown to be of great value in relieving pain or even curing a wide variety of ailments. Western medicine does not yet understand how acupuncture works, but there seems little doubt that it can be of great benefit.

CHINESE AMERICANS IN THE ARTS

Literature and the movies are two other areas in which Chinese Americans have made their mark. Maxine Hong Kingston was one of the first Chinese authors to succeed in the mainstream media. Her book, *The Woman Warrior: Memoir of a Girlhood Among Ghosts*, won the National Book Critics award for non-fiction in 1976. Amy Tan's *The Joy Luck Club* was a popular mainstream novel and a Hollywood movie in 1993. Director Wayne Wang directed not only *The Joy Luck Club* but also a number of other critically acclaimed movies. Like Wang, Ang Lee has also carved out a successful career as a movie director. Among his more well-known movies are *The Wedding Banquet* and *Sense and Sensibility*, which was based on a Jane Austen novel.

Action-movie director John Woo has had great success with movies such as *Broken Arrow* and *Face Off*. Bruce Lee, perhaps the greatest action-movie hero of all time, helped to change the inaccurate image of Chinese males as polite and passive victims. Ironically, Lee was once considered for the lead role in a TV show called *Kung Fu*. The reason he did not get the part was because the show's producers decided audiences would not accept an Asian American as a hero.

Architecture is another area in which Chinese Americans

Chinese-American movie director Ang Lee holds up his Best Director award for his film *Crouching Tiger, Hidden Dragon* at the Hong Kong Film Presentation Ceremony in 2001. Lee also directed *The Wedding Banquet* and a film adaptation of Jane Austen's *Sense and Sensibility*.

have made major contributions. I. M. Pei is one of this country's most famed architects. Among his most well-known buildings are the East Wing of the National Gallery of Art in Washington, the John F. Kennedy Library in Boston, and the Rock and Roll Hall of Fame in Cleveland.

One of the most simple but elegant structures erected in the last 30 years was designed by a young Chinese-American college student named Maya Lin. Since its dedication in 1982, her Vietnam Veterans Memorial has helped heal the wounds of the Vietnam War for hundreds of thousands of Americans. Meanwhile, Lin has gone on to design other memorials, including the Civil Rights Memorial in Montgomery, Alabama.

Notable Chinese Americans

I. M. Pei (1917–) Born in Canton, China, Pei earned his master's degree at Harvard University. His widely-known abstract designs and eye-catching monumental buildings include a wing of the National Gallery of Art in Washington, the John F. Kennedy Library in Boston, and the Bank of China in Hong Kong, one of the world's tallest buildings.

Tsung-Dao Lee (1926–) After going to college in China, Lee earned his doctorate in physics from University of Chicago in 1950. He then reunited with Chen Ning Yang, with whom he attended school in China, while working at Princeton University. The two men won the Nobel Prize for solving a problem in particle physics that had mystified scientists for years. Lee went on to receive many other honors and awards in astrophysics, mechanics, and hydrodynamics.

Maxine Hong Kingston (1940–) Born in Stockton, California, Kingston played a crucial role in introducing Asian-American literature to a wider audience. The daughter of first-generation immigrants from China, her work details the challenges of children caught between old and new ways. Two of her books, *The Woman Warrior: Memoirs of a Girlhood Among Ghosts* and *China Men*, won National Book Critics Circle Awards.

Bruce Lee (1940–1972) Though born in San Francisco in 1940 when his father, an opera singer, was on tour, Lee was raised in Hong Kong. He appeared in over 20 movies by his teens. At one time the highest-paid movie star in the world, Lee became the world's number one exponent of martial arts. He greatly increased awareness of Chinese fighting arts and philosophies. He studied for a philosophy doctorate at the University of Washington before dying mysteriously at the age of 32.

Connie Chung (1946–) Born in Washington, D.C., Chung graduated from the University of Maryland and started her career as a copy person at WTTG-TV in Washington, D.C., in 1969. After working as a news writer, then news reporter, CBS hired Chung as a national correspondent in 1971. She left CBS for other networks, but returned in 1989. After her stint as a news anchor, she became a fellow at Harvard's John F. Kennedy School of Government in 1997. In 2002, CNN offered Chung her own news program, "Connie Chung Tonight."

Notable Chinese Americans *(continued)*

Ang Lee (1954–) After failing the college entrance examinations in his native Taiwan, Lee moved to the United States in 1978. At the University of Illinois, he attended the theater arts program. Lee's acclaimed film for his master's degree from New York University, *Fine Line*, allowed him to direct other films. His films, *Pushing Hands, The Wedding Banquet* and *Eat, Drink, Man, Woman*, explored the conflicts between different generations of Chinese Americans. They received both critical and commercial praise. Lee has also skillfully directed movies, *Sense and Sensibility* and *The Ice Storm*, with non-Asian themes.

Yo-Yo Ma (1955–) An accomplished cellist, Ma gave his first public recital at age five. Born in Paris, France, Ma debuted at Carnegie Hall when he was only nine. After studying at the Juilliard School of Music, he attended Harvard University. Internationally known for his classical recordings, Ma has won several Grammy awards and continues to make new and adventurous music.

Maya Lin (1959–) Born in Athens, Ohio, Maya Lin attended Yale University. For her senior thesis project in 1981, she submitted a design for a national contest for the Vietnam Veteran's Memorial. From over 1,400 entries, her simple but elegant design of two polished walls of black granite set in a "V" and inscribed with the names of the 58,000 dead or missing veterans of that war was chosen. Her memorial has deeply moved hundreds of thousands of Americans and helped heal the wounds of the Vietnam War.

Michelle Kwan (1980–) Born in 1980 in Torrance, California, Michelle Kwan is one of the most popular American figure skaters. At the age of 13, she was an alternate to the Olympics in 1994. She has been U.S. National Champion six times and a World Champion four times. She won a silver medal in the 1998 Olympics and a bronze medal in the 2002 Olympics.

CHINESE AMERICANS IN SCIENCE

The number of Chinese Americans who have excelled in the sciences are too numerous to mention. Among them are Nobel Prize winners Tsung-Dao Lee and Chen Ning Yan (for their discoveries in particle physics) and Yuan T. Lee (for his work in chemistry). At least two Chinese Americans have become major generals (one in the air force and the other in the army), while another, Gary Locke, was elected governor of Washington State in 1996.

CHINESE WORK ETHIC

Perhaps the greatest contribution Chinese Americans have made to America is their attitude toward work. There is a long tradition in China that work is noble and that a job worth doing is worth doing well. From the building of the Transcontinental Railroad, to the digging of irrigation systems to the tending of California's first vineyards, Chinese immigrants exemplified a belief in the value of honest work. In so doing, they helped civilize the "Wild West" in a way that was desperately needed. As Franklin Tuthill, author of *History of California*, put it:

> [The Chinese] panned gold, opened up mines, brought in timber to build houses on land they reclaimed. They opened up the vineyards and rich farmlands.
>
> They added dignity and discipline, order and wealth to a frontier land that when they came was not yet a state, not yet a community of law and order. They helped to link it with the rest of the continent and so make possible its greater settlement. . . . The cleanliness, politeness and good behavior of the Chinese was on everybody's mouth and what they contributed saved several counties from bankruptcy.

Chinese Americans have much to be proud of. For many, like Tung Pok Chin, who arrived in the United States in 1934, maintaining his family's Chinese traditions was equally as important as learning American ones. "Our Chinese New Year's Eve dinner together would have as much significance as the Thanksgiving holiday," he recalled, "and our New Year's celebration would be as important as the American New Year's Day, the first of January. We were Americans, but we would always be *Chinese* Americans."

CHINESE NEW YEAR

The traditional Chinese New Year celebration is a time of great excitement and joy in Chinese communities. The festivities

Red envelopes containing "lucky" money are given to children in celebration of the Chinese New Year. The evening ends with fireworks that frighten off evil spirits and honor the gods. These traditions encourage the year to start with happiness and prosperity.

begin 22 days before the New Year (which is based on the lunar calendar and begins in January or February) and last for 15 days afterward. Beforehand, people buy and prepare special food, thoroughly clean their houses, and throw out unwanted items so that the coming year will begin fresh and clean. Everything possible is done to begin the year on a prosperous, happy note.

New Year's Eve is the high point of the season. If possible, every family member tries to make it home to share in the traditional holiday meal. Children receive red envelopes containing "lucky" money. Midnight is greeted with a thunderous roar of firecrackers and exploding skyrockets meant to frighten off evil spirits and honor the gods. The fireworks continue long into the night and begin again after daylight. Colorful dragon and lion dances are also a part of the traditional Chinese New Year's celebration.

Such vibrant festivities are a fitting tribute to the resilient spirit of the thousands of courageous Chinese who helped build the United States. They suffered decades of discrimination but persevered long enough to see the nation finally begin to live up to its ideals. Their considerable achievements help reaffirm what America is all about.

1565–1815	Chinese sailors work aboard cargo ships that travel regularly between the Philippines and Mexico.
1785	Three Chinese sailors are stranded in Baltimore for a year when the captain of their ship, the *Pallas*, leaves to get married. This is the earliest record of Chinese in the continental United States.
1818	First group of Chinese foreign students arrives in United States.
1848	Gold is discovered at Sutter's Mill in California.
1849	Records indicate 780 Chinese living in the San Francisco Bay area of California.
1850	California courts rule that Chinese cannot be allowed to testify against white persons (in 1854 the ruling is upheld by U.S. Court of Appeals).
1852	Estimated Chinese population in California is 20,000.
1854	The California Foreign Miners Tax is amended so it applies only to Chinese. For the next 20 years, the tax makes up half the total tax revenue for the state.
1855	Yung Wing gets a degree from Yale. He is the first Chinese to graduate from a U.S. college. That same year, California declares public schools will admit white children only.
1865	First Chinese begin working on Transcontinental Railroad. Upon its completion in 1869, Chinese laborers go on to help build the Canadian Pacific, the Northern Pacific, the Southern Pacific, and most of the railroads from Texas to Alaska.
1868	The Fourteenth Amendment to the U.S. Constitution states that a person born in the United States is a U.S. citizen by birth, but such rights are not extended to Chinese until a Supreme Court case in 1898.
1877	Amid increasing anti-Chinese sentiment on the West Coast, the Workingmen's Party of California pressures politicians to exclude Chinese from America and popularizes the slogan, "The Chinese Must Go!"
1879	California's second Constitution declares Chinese an "undesirable" race to be excluded from the state.
1882	After intense lobbying by California politicians, Congress passes the Chinese Exclusion Act. It bans all Chinese laborers from the United States for 10 years.
1888	The Scott Act denies re-entry to 20,000 Chinese visiting overseas, even though they possess valid re-entry permits.

1892   The Geary Act extends the Chinese Exclusion Act for another 10 years (such extensions will keep the act in effect until 1943). The law also requires Chinese in the United States to register with the government for a certificate of identity or risk arrest and deportation.

1895   The Native Sons of the Golden State organize to fight for Chinese-American civil rights. They later become the Chinese American Citizens Alliance.

1905   In a protest against the treatment of Chinese in the United States, the government of China organizes a boycott of American goods.

1906   After an earthquake and fire devastate San Francisco and destroy numerous government records, many Chinese take advantage of the situation to claim native (U.S.) birthrights. As "paper sons and daughters," they become citizens.

1910   The Angel Island Immigration Station begins operation in San Francisco Bay. During its 30 years of operation, 175,000 Chinese were detained there.

1924   The Asian Exclusion Act bans immigration of all aliens ineligible for U.S. citizenship (the Chinese). It also bans Chinese wives of U.S. citizens from joining their husbands in the United States.

1930   Congress amends 1924 law to allow entry of wives of U.S. citizens who had married prior to 1924.

1941   After Japan attacks Pearl Harbor, China becomes a U.S. ally against Japan. Many Chinese Americans join the armed forces or work in the defense industry.

1943   The Chinese Exclusion Acts are repealed and an annual immigration quota of 105 Chinese is established.

1947   The War Brides Act is changed to allow wives of Chinese-American war veterans to immigrate to the United States on a non-quota basis.

1949   After the Chinese Communist Party defeats the Chinese Nationalist Party on the battlefield and takes control of China, 5,000 Chinese students are allowed to stay in United States. Meanwhile, the Nationalist government establishes headquarters on the island of Taiwan.

1959   Hiram Fong of Hawaii becomes first Chinese American elected to the U.S. Senate.

1965 Amidst the growing cry for civil rights reform in the United States, the 1965 Immigration Act allows the large-scale immigration of Chinese families to the United States for the first time. It officially takes effect in 1968.

1972 Relations between mainland China and the United States improve dramatically after President Nixon visits the People's Republic of China.

1981 The 1965 Immigration Act is modified so that both Taiwan and mainland China have a yearly quota of 20,000 immigrants.

1990 The 1965 Immigration Act is modified to encourage those with special skills to become U.S. citizens.

1992 Because of the Tianneman Square Massacre, Congress passes the Chinese Student Protection Act. It allows 48,212 students from mainland China to remain in the United States permanently.

Ambrose, Stephen. *Nothing Like It in the World*. New York: Simon & Schuster, 2000.

Barth, Gunther. *Bitter Strength: A History of the Chinese in the United States, 1850–1870*. Cambridge, MA: Harvard University Press, 1964.

Bonner, Arthur. *Alas! What Brought Thee Hither? The Chinese in New York, 1800-1950*. Madison, NJ: Fairleigh Dickinson University Press, 1997.

Carter, Alden R. *China Past—China Future*. New York: Franklin Watts, 1994.

Chan, Sucheng. *Entry Denied*. Philadelphia: Temple University Press, 1991.

Chang, Leslie. *Beyond the Narrow Gate*. New York: Dutton, 1999.

Chen, Jack. *The Chinese of America*. San Francisco: Harper & Row, 1980.

Chen, Jerome. *China and the West*. Bloomington, IN: Indiana University Press, 1979.

Chin, Tung Pok with Winifred C. Chin. *Paper Son: One Man's Story*. Philadelphia: Temple University Press, 2000.

Choy, Phillip P., Lorraine Dong, and Marlon K. Hom. *Coming Man: 19th Century American Perceptions of the Chinese*. Seattle: University of Washington Press, 1994.

Fong-Torres, Ben. *The Rice Room*. New York: Penguin Books, 1994.

Green, Robert. *China*. San Diego: Lucent Books, 1999.

Gyory, Andrew. *Closing the Gate: Race, Politics and the Chinese Exclusion Act*. Chapel Hill, NC: University of North Carolina Press, 1998.

Hall, Edward. *Tea That Burns*. New York: The Free Press, 1998.

Hom, Marlon K. *Songs of Gold Mountain*. Berkeley, CA: University of California Press, 1987.

Hoexter, Corinne K. *From Canton to California*. New York: Four Winds Press, 1976.

Hsu, Madeline Yuan-yin. *Dreaming of Gold, Dreaming of Home*. Stanford, CA: Stanford University Press, 2000.

Kingston, Maxine Hong. *The Woman Warrior: Memoirs of a Girlhood Among Ghosts*. New York: Alfred A. Knopf, 1975.

Ling, Huping. *Surviving on Gold Mountain*. Albany, NY: State University of New York Press, 1998.

Loo, Chalsa M. *Chinatown: Most Time, Hard Time*. New York: Praeger, 1991.

Major, John S. *The Land and People of China.* New York: JB Lippincott, 1989.

Mar, M. Elaine. *Paper Daughter: A Memoir.* New York: HarperCollins, 1999.

McCunn, Ruthanne Lum. *An Illustrated History of the Chinese in America.* San Francisco: Design Enterprises of San Francisco, 1979.

McCunn, Ruthanne Lum. *Chinese American Portraits: Personal Histories 1828–1988.* San Francisco: Chronicle Books, 1988.

Morrison, Joan and Charlotte Fox Zaabusky. *Mosaic: the Immigrant Experience in the Words of Those Who Lived It.* Pittsburgh: University of Pittsburgh Press, 1980.

Pan, Lynn. *Sons of the Yellow Emperor: A History of the Chinese Diaspora.* Boston: Little, Brown, 1990.

Lyman, Stanford. *Chinese Americans.* New York: Random House, 1974.

Russell, Don, ed. *Trails of the Iron Horse: An Informal History by The Western Writers of America.* Garden City, NY: Doubleday, 1975.

Steiner, Stan. *Fusang: The Chinese Who Built America.* New York: Harper & Row, 1979.

Takaki, Ronald. *A Different Mirror: A History of Multicultural America.* Boston: Little, Brown, 1993.

Takaki, Ronald. *Iron Cages: Race and Culture in 19th-Century America.* New York: Oxford University Press, 1990.

Takaki, Ronald. *Strangers from a Different Shore.* New York: Penguin Books, 1989.

Tong, Benson. *The Chinese Americans.* Westport, CT: Greenwood Press, 2000.

FICTION

Jen, Gish. *Typical American.* Boston: Houghton Mifflin, 1991.

Kingston, Maxine Hong. *The Woman Warrior: Memoirs of a Girlhood Among Ghosts.* New York: Alfred A. Knopf, 1975.

Ng, Fae Myenne. *Bone.* New York: Hyperion, 1993.

Tan, Amy. *The Joy Luck Club.* New York: Vintage Books, 1991.

NONFICTION

Chin, Tung Pok with Winifred C. Chin. *Paper Son: One Man's Story.* Philadelphia: Temple University Press, 2000.

Fong-Torres, Ben. *The Rice Room.* New York: Penguin Books, 1994.

Khu, Josephine M.T., ed. *Cultural Curiosity: Thirteen Stories about the Search for Chinese Roots.* Berkeley, California: University of California Press, 2001.

Mar, M. Elaine. *Paper Daughter: A Memoir.* New York: HarperCollins, 1999.

She, Colleen, ed. *Refugees from China Speak Out (In Their Own Voices).* New York: Rosen Publishing Group, 1995.

Angel Island Immigration Station
www.angelisland.org/immigr02.html

Angel Island: Journeys Remembered by Chinese Houstonians
www.chron.com/content/chronicle/special/angelisland/intro.html

Chinese Immigration to the United States, 1851–1900
http://memory.loc.gov/ammem/ndlpedu/features/timeline/riseind/chinimms/
  chinimms.html

Discovering China: Movers and Shakers
http://library.thinkquest.org/26469/movers-and-shakers/?tqskip1=1&tqtime=0522

Immigration and Naturalization Service: Chinese Immigrant Files
http://www.ins.usdoj.gov/graphics/aboutins/history/chinese.htm

Angel Island Immigration Station Foundation
330 Townsend Street, Suite 235
San Francisco, CA 94107

China Institute in America
125 East 65th Street
New York, NY 10021

Immigration and Naturalization Service (INS) Historian
425 I Street NW, Room 1100
Washington, DC 20536

Organization of Chinese Americans
1001 Connecticut Ave., NW, Suite #601
Washington, DC 20036

San Diego Chinese Historical Society
404 Third Avenue
San Diego, CA 92101

Acceptance into America, 23, 82-88
  and assimilation, 23, 82-83
  and citizenship, 19, 79, 86
  and incomes, 87-88
  and lifting immigration restrictions,
    19, 21-22, 76, 79, 85-86
  and marriage to Chinese, 19, 21, 79
  and occupations, 81
  and schools, 79, 81, 82, 87
  and settlement patterns, 81, 82, 86
  and Supreme Court, 72
  and WWII, 76-79
Acupuncture, 23, 91
Agriculture, Chinese working in,
  52-54
Altars (joss house), 68
American Federation of Labor, 58
Angel Island, 73-75
Anti-Chinese sentiment, 19, 56-67
  and Chinese as opium addicts, 67
  and Chinese as scapegoats, 58-60
  and Chinese carrying disease and
    filth, 67, 72
  and citizenship, 19, 58, 61
  and courts, 19, 54-55, 72
  and detention at Angel Island,
    73-75
  and identity cards, 72
  and Irish railroad workers, 17
  and land ownership, 19, 60
  and legal harassment, 71-76
  and marriage to Chinese, 19, 21
  and myths about the Chinese,
    65-66
  and non-recognition, 18-19, 54
  and political maneuvers, 60-61
  and restrictions on immigration,
    19, 61, 71-73, 75-76, 82
  and riots, 19, 50-52, 60, 61, 62-64,
    67
  and schools, 64
  and settlement locations, 19
  and union membership, 19, 58, 60
  and voting rights, 19
  and white gold miners, 49-52

Architecture, and Chinese, 91-93
Artisans, in Chinese social structure,
  28, 30
Arts, and Chinese, 91
Assimilation, 23, 82-83
Australia, 42

Balmoral, 42
Britain, 31, 39
Businesses, Chinese in, 64, 90

California, Chinese in
  and agricultural work, 52-54
  and anti-Chinese sentiment, 58-61,
    62, 64, 72, 73-75
  and Chinatowns, 60, 61, 62, 72
  and detention at Angel Island,
    73-75
  and employment restrictions, 61
  and gold mining, 14, 32-33, 34, 36,
    49-52, 56, 90
  and injustice to Chinese, 54-55
  journey to, 39-40, 42-43
  and land reclamation, 54
  and San Francisco earthquake,
    73, 75
  and schools, 64
  and support system for emigrants,
    45-46, 48-49
Canning industries, and Chinese,
  53-54
Canton, emigration from, 38
Cape Horn, and Central Pacific
  Railroad, 15-17
Caribbean, 39, 65-66
Central Pacific Railroad, 14-17
Chap, G., 42
Children
  and paper sons and daughters,
    73, 74
  and schools, 79, 81, 82, 87
  and smuggled into U.S., 73, 74,
    75-76
Chin, Tung Pok, 69, 95
China, 24-33, 82

and ban on emigration, 37
and boycott of American goods, 73
and class system, 27
and corruption and poverty, 30-31
and early history, 25-26
and Great Wall, 26-27
and isolation, 26, 27
and language, 27
and physical features, 24-25
and religion, 30
and social structure, 28-30, 46
as U.S. ally in WWII, 76-79
and war between Communists and Nationalists, 81-82
and wars and rebellions, 31-32, 36
Chinatowns, 55, 60, 61, 62, 63, 72, 87
Chinese-American Citizens' Alliance, 75
Chinese Exclusion Act, 61
Chinese language, 89-90
Chinese New Year, 68-69, 82, 95, 97
Chinese theater, 67
Chinese traditions/culture, 23, 67-69
  and food, 23, 90
  and gambling, 67
  and health, 23, 91
  and holidays, 68-69, 82, 95, 97
  presentation of, 82, 95
  and religion, 23, 30, 68
  and schools, 82
  and splits among Chinese, 88-89
  and theater, 67
Citizenship, and Chinese, 19, 58, 61, 79, 86
Cleveland, Grover, 62
Cold War, 82
Confucius/Confucianism, 30
Coolies, 39, 65
Courts, and Chinese, 19, 54-55, 72
Credit ticket system, 40
Crocker, Charles, 14-15, 18, 52
Cuba, 39, 65-66

Defense industry, Chinese in, 79
Domestic help, Chinese as, 64

Emperors, 26
English language, 89-90
Exclusion Act of 1882, 19, 71-72
Factories, Chinese in, 56

Family
  in China, 28, 37
  in U.S., 48, 76, 79, 82, 87-90
Farmers, in Chinese social structure, 28, 30
Fishing industry, Chinese in, 54
Fongs, 48
Fong-Torres, Ben, 89
Food, 23, 90
Forced labor, Chinese doing, 39, 65-66

Gambling, by Chinese, 67
GI Bill of Rights, 79
Gold Rush
  and Chinese miners, 32-33, 49-52, 90
  and emigration from China, 14, 32-33, 34, 36, 37, 56
Great Wall of China, 26-27
Guangdong, emigration from, 33, 34-36, 42, 69, 88

Hak-chan, 38-39
Hall, George W., 54-55
Han Chinese, 27
Hawaii, 21, 86-87
Hayes, Rutherford B., 60-61
Health traditions, and Chinese, 23, 91
Holidays, 68-69
Homesickness, of emigrants, 42-43, 48
Hong Kong, emigration from, 38, 88
Hui kuans (mutual aid societies)
  in China, 28-29
  in U.S., 46, 48, 72

Identity cards, Chinese carrying, 72
Immigration Act of 1924, 75-76
Immigration and Nationality Act,
    85-86
Immigration to America
    after WWII, 21-22
    and Cold War, 82
    and deportation, 74
    easing restrictions on, 19, 21-22,
        76, 79, 85-86
    and Gold Rush, 14, 32-33, 34, 36,
        37
    from Guangdong, 33, 34-36, 42,
        69, 88
    and Nationalist defeat in China,
        81-82
    and number of Chinese, 21-22, 56,
        58, 61-62, 75
    and parachute kids, 90
    and political turmoil, 31-32, 36
    and poverty, 13, 30-33, 34, 36-37
    quotas on, 79, 85-86
    restrictions on, 19, 61, 71-73,
        75-76, 82
    and returning home, 37, 46, 55,
        61, 62, 64
    and smuggling of wives and
        children, 73, 74
    and splits among Chinese, 88-90
    and women, 79
    by young, married men, 36-37,
        63-64, 73, 75-76
    See also California
Income, and Chinese family, 87-88
Influence of Chinese, 23, 90-95
    and arts, 91-93
    and Chinese New Year, 68-69, 82,
        95, 97
    and Chinese work ethic, 95
    and food, 23, 90
    and health traditions, 23, 91
    and number of Chinese, 22-23, 75,
        85, 86-87
    and science, 94
    and West, 13-19, 52-54, 56, 95

Irish railroad workers, versus Chinese
    workers, 17

Johnson, Lyndon B., 21-22
Journey to America, 38-40, 42-43
    and detention at Angel Island,
        73-75
    and forced labor, 39, 65-66
    and homesickness, 42-43
    money for, 39-40, 46, 65-66
    and port cities, 38-39
    ships for, 39-40, 42

Kahn, Florence, 75-76
Kearney, Denis, 59
Kingston, Maxine Hong, 91
Kin, Huie, 40, 42, 61

Land ownership, and Chinese, 19, 60
Land reclamation, and Chinese, 54
Lao Zi, 30
Laundries, Chinese owning, 64
Lee, Ang, 91
Lee, Bruce, 91
Lee, Tsung-Dao, 94
Lee, Yuan T., 94
Libertad, 42
Lin, Maya, 92-93
Literature, and Chinese, 91
Locke, Gary, 94

Macao, emigration from, 38
Mainland China, emigration from, 88
Mandarin, 86
Marriage to Chinese, 19, 21, 79
Merchants
    in China, 28, 30, 46
    in U.S., 45-46, 48, 49
Miners, Chinese as, 32-33, 49-52, 90
Ming, Chum, 32-33
Movies, and Chinese, 91

Occupations, 13-19, 32-33, 49-54, 56,
    61, 64, 79, 81, 82, 86, 87, 88, 90,
    91-94, 95

Opium addicts, Chinese as, 67
Opium Wars, 31
Organizations
    hui kuans (mutual aid societies),
        28-29, 46, 48
    tongs (secret societies), 29-30, 31,
        48

Paper sons and daughters, 73, 74
Parachute kids, 90
Pearl Harbor, 76
Pei, I. M., 92
Pigpens, 39
Political involvement, 94
    and citizenship, 19, 79, 86
    and WWII, 76-78
Political turmoil, and emigration,
    31-32, 36
Port cities, emigration from, 38
Poverty, and emigration, 13, 30-33,
    34, 36-37
Professional jobs, Chinese in, 82, 86,
    87
Promontory, Utah, and
    Transcontinental Railroad, 17-18

Qing Dynasty, 26, 30-32, 37

Railroads, and Chinese, 13-19, 52, 56
Raisin industry, Chinese in, 53
Ranches, Chinese working on, 52
Religion, 30, 68
Restaurants, Chinese owning, 64, 90
Robertson, J.B., 42
Roosevelt, Franklin, 73, 79

Scholar officials, in Chinese social
    structure, 28
Schools
    in California, 48
    Chinese in, 82, 87
    discrimination against Chinese in,
        64
    and GI Bill of Rights, 79, 81
    and splits among Chinese, 88

Science, and Chinese, 94
Scott Act, 71-72
Scurvy, from journey to U.S., 42
Settlement patterns
    and Chinatowns, 55, 60, 61, 62, 63,
        72, 87
    outside Chinatowns, 81, 82, 86
    and splits among Chinese, 88
Seymour, Horatio, 59
Shang Dynasty, 26
Shanghaied, 39, 65-66
Shen, Yeh Ming, 36
Ships, for journey to U.S., 39-40, 42
Ship's fever, from journey to U.S., 42
Sierra Nevada, and Central Pacific
    Railroad, 14-17
Six Companies, 46, 72
Slot racket, 73, 74
Small businesses, Chinese owning,
    64, 90
South America, 39, 65-66
Spain, 39
State government, Chinese barred
    from working in, 61
Steerage, 40, 42
Strobridge, James, 15
Summit Tunnel, 16
Supreme Court, and Chinese, 72

Tai chi, 91
Taipeng Revolution, 36
Taiwan, emigration from, 88
Tan, Amy, 91
Taoism, 23, 30
Technical jobs, Chinese in, 82, 86,
    87
Tilden, Samuel J., 60
Tongs (secret societies), 29-30, 31,
    48
Tong wars, 49
Transcontinental Railroad, 13-19,
    52

Unemployment, and Chinese, 57-60
Union Pacific Railroad, 17

Unions, Chinese barred from, 19, 58, 60

Vineyards, Chinese in, 53
Voting rights, and Chinese, 19

Wang, Wayne, 91
War Brides Act of 1945, 21, 79
West
    and anti-Chinese riots, 62-64
    Chinese contributions to, 13-19, 52-54, 56, 95

Women
    and emigration to U.S., 79
    and remaining in China, 36-37, 63
    and smuggled into U.S., 73, 74, 75-76
Woo, John, 91
Work ethic, of Chinese, 95
    See also Occupations
World War II, 76-79

Yan, Chen Ning, 94
Yellow Peril, 59, 87

page:

13: © Josef Scaylea/Corbis
18: Associated Press, Union Pacific
21: © Bettmann/Corbis
23: © Bob Krist/Corbis
25: © Joseph Sohm, ChromosSohm, Inc./
    Corbis
29: © Julia Waterlow; Eye Ubiquitous/
    Corbis
32: © Corbis
35: © The Purcell Team/Corbis
38: Hierophant Collection
43: © Hulton-Deutsch Collection/Corbis
45: © Bettmann/Corbis
48: © Corbis

51: © Bettmann/Corbis
53: © Corbis
57: © Corbis
63: © Bettmann/Corbis
65: © Bettmann/Corbis
68: © Corbis
71: © Bettmann/Corbis
77: National Archives
78: Library of Congress
81: © Minnesota Historical Society/Corbis
85: © Phil Schermeister/Corbis
89: Associated Press, AP
92: Associated Press, AP
96: © Phil Schermeister/Corbis

Frontis: Courtesy University of Texas at Austin, Perry-Castañeda Map Collection, CIA map.

MICHAEL MARTIN is a freelance writer and former editor at *Reminisce* magazine who now lives on a bluff above the Mississippi River in Lansing, Iowa. He is the author of a half-dozen books for children along with numerous magazine articles for both adults and children. This is his first book for Chelsea House Publishers.

DANIEL PATRICK MOYNIHAN is a former United States senator from New York. He is also the only person in American history to have served in the cabinets or subcabinets of four successive presidents—Kennedy, Johnson, Nixon, and Ford. Formerly a professor of government at Harvard University, he has written and edited many books.